TABLE OF CONTENTS

HOW TO PREPARE FOR THE EXAM...	3
HOW TO STUDY..	3
WHAT TO STUDY..	4
HELPFUL HINTS...	4
REGULATIONS AT THE EXAMINATION SITE...............................	5
TYPICAL EXAMINATION QUESTIONS..	6
USEFUL FORMULAS	9
EXAM 1 – JOURNEYMAN QUESTIONS..	13
EXAM 2 – JOURNEYMAN QUESTIONS	19
EXAM 3 – JOURNEYMAN QUESTIONS	27
EXAM 4 – JOURNEYMAN QUESTIONS	34
EXAM 5 – JOURNEYMAN QUESTIONS	41
EXAM 6 – JOURNEYMAN QUESTIONS	47
EXAM 7 – MASTERS QUESTIONS	54
EXAM 8 – MASTERS QUESTIONS	61
EXAM 9 – MASTERS QUESTIONS	68
EXAM 10 – MASTERS QUESTIONS	75
FINAL EXAM – JOURNEYMAN AND MASTERS QUESTIONS	82

EXAM 1 SOLUTIONS	**108**
EXAM 2 SOLUTIONS...	**112**
EXAM 3 SOLUTIONS...	**117**
EXAM 4 SOLUTIONS...	**122**
EXAM 5 SOLUTIONS...	**127**
EXAM 6 SOLUTIONS...	**132**
EXAM 7 SOLUTIONS...	**137**
EXAM 8 SOLUTIONS...	**142**
EXAM 9 SOLUTIONS...	**148**
EXAM 10 SOLUTIONS...	**154**
FINAL EXAM SOLUTIONS..	**159**

PREFACE

HOW TO PREPARE FOR THE EXAM

This book is a guide to preparing for the electricians' exam. It will not make you a competent electrician, nor teach you the electrical trade, but it will give you an idea of the type of questions asked on most electricians' examinations.

Most electrical exams consist of multiple-choice questions and this is the type of questions reflected in this exam guide. These questions will give you a feel for how many of the examinations nationwide are structured. These questions are an example of the many questions the author has encountered when taking numerous exams in recent years.

Begin your pre-exam preparation with two points in mind.

- Opportunities in life will arise – be prepared for them.
- The more you LEARN – the more you EARN.

Attempting to take an exam without preparation is a complete waste of time. Attend classes at your local community college. Attend seminars, electrical code updates and company sponsored programs. Many major electrical suppliers and local unions sponsored classes of this type at no cost. Take advantage of them.

Become familiar with the National Electrical Code®; the Code has a LANGUAGE all its own. Understanding the language will help one to better interpret the NEC®. Do not become intimidated by its length. Become thoroughly familiar with definitions in Chapter One, if you don't, the remainder of the NEC® will be difficult to comprehend. Remember, on the job we use different "lingo" and phrases compared to the way the NEC® is written and to the way many test questions are expressed.

HOW TO STUDY

Before beginning to study, get into the right frame of mind, be relaxed. Study in a quiet place that is conducive to learning. If such a place is not available, go to your local library. It is important that you have a quiet, relaxed atmosphere in which to study.

It is much better to study many short lengths of time than attempt to study fewer, longer lengths of time. Try to study a little while, say about an hour, every evening. You will need the support and understanding of your family to set aside this much needed time.

As you study this exam preparation book and other references, highlight important points with a highlighter. This makes it easier to locate Code references when taking the exam.

Use a straight edge, such as a six inch ruler when using the NEC® tables and charts. A very common mistake is to get on the wrong line when using these tables; if this happens, the result is an incorrect answer.

Use tabs on the major sections of your NEC®, this makes it easier and takes less time to locate these major sections when taking the exam. The national average allowed per question is approximately three minutes; you cannot waste time.

WHAT TO STUDY

A common reason for one to be unsuccessful when attempting to pass the electricians' exam, is not knowing what to study. In this book we will address the most common type of questions you will encounter on most calculations examinations.

The subject matter covered in most electrical calculations examinations is:

- Power and current formulas
- Branch circuit loads
- Cooking equipment demand loads
- Appliance demand loads
- Conductor ampacity and sizing
- One-family dwelling services
- Multifamily dwelling services
- Commercial loads and services
- Raceway fill and sizing
- Box fill and sizing
- Voltage drop
- Motor branch circuits and feeders
- Motor overload and overcurrent protection

Become very familiar with questions on the above referenced subject matter. Knowing what to study is a major step to passing your exam.

HELPFUL HINTS ON TAKING THE EXAM

1. <u>Complete the easy questions and "gimmies" first</u>. On most tests, all questions are valued the same. If you become too frustrated on any one question, it may reflect upon your entire test.

2. <u>Keep track of time</u>. Do not spend too much time on one question. If a question is difficult for you, mark on the answer sheet the answer you think is correct and place a check (√) by that question in the examination booklet. Then go on the next question; of you have time after finishing the rest of the exam, you can go back to the question, guess. Choose the answer that is most familiar to you. In most cases, the answer is B or C.

3. <u>Only change answers if you know you are right</u>. Usually, your first answer is your best answer.

4. <u>Relax</u>. Do not get uptight and stressed out when testing.

5. <u>Tab your Code Book</u>. References are easier and faster to find.

Copyright 2016   BrownTechnical.org

6. <u>Use a straight edge</u>. Prevent getting on the wrong line when referring to the tables in the NEC®.

7. <u>Get a good nights rest before the exam</u>. Do not attempt to drive several hours to an exam site, be rested and alert.

8. <u>Understand the question</u>. One key word in a question can make a difference in what the question is asking. Underlining key words in the question will help you to understand the meaning of the question.

9. <u>Use a dependable calculator</u>. Use a solar powered calculator that has a battery back-up. Many test sites are not well lighted; this type of calculator will prepare you for such a situation. Perhaps, bring along a spare calculator.

10. <u>Show up at least 30 minutes prior to your exam time</u>. You may allow yourself even more time for traffic, etc.

TYPICAL REGULATIONS AT THE PLACE OF EXAMINATION

To ensure that all examinees are examined under equally favorable conditions, the following regulations and procedures are observed at most examination sites:

1. Each examinee must present proper photo identification, preferably his/her driver's license before he/she will be permitted to take the examination.

2. No cameras, notes, tape recorders, pagers or cellular phones are allowed in the examination room.

3. No one will be permitted to work beyond the established time limits.

4. Typically, examinees are not permitted any reference material EXCEPT the National Electrical Code®.

5. Examinees will be permitted to use noiseless calculators during the examination. Calculators which provide programmable ability or pre-programmed calculators are prohibited.

6. Permission of an examination proctor must be obtained before leaving the room while the examination is in progress.

7. Each examinee is assigned to a seat specifically designated by name and/or number when admitted to the examination room.

TYPICAL EXAMINATION QUESTIONS

The examples on this page are intended to illustrate typical questions that will appear on most electricians' exams.

EXAMPLE 1

A single-phase, 240-volt, 7,500 VA electric fryer is to be installed in a restaurant. What load, in amperes, will the fryer draw?

    A. 20.80 amperes
    B. 31.25 amperes
    C. 62.50 amperes
    D. 27.50 amperes

Here you are asked to determine the current flow in the conductors serving the fryer using the information given. Power is expressed as 7,500 VA and voltage is 240. The formula to be used is I = P/E. Substitute the values given;
I = 7,500 VA ÷ 240 volts = 31.25 amperes; the answer is **B**.

EXAMPLE 2

A single-phase, 240-volt, 5 hp, Design B, 40°C rise motor has a FLA rating of 25 amperes indicated on the nameplate. The MINIMUM rating of the overload device used to protect this motor as required by the NEC® is _____.

    A. 32.50 amperes
    B. 28.25 amperes
    C. 31.25 amperes
    D. 35.00 amperes

Here the "question" is in the form of an incomplete statement. You task is to select the choice that best completes the statement. In this case, you should have selected **C** since Section 430.6(A)(2) of the NEC® specifies motor overload protection shall be based on the motor nameplate rating and Section 430.32(A)(1) specifies the overload device shall be selected to trip at a value of not more than 125% of the motor nameplate full-load current rating, if the motor has a marked temperature rise of not over 40° C. FLA = 25 amperes x 125% = 31.25 amperes

EXAMPLE 3

Taking all exceptions into consideration, the largest standard size inverse time circuit breaker permitted to provide short-circuit, branch-circuit and ground-fault protection for a 5 hp, 230-volt, single-phase, continuous-duty motor has a standard rating of _____.

    A. 110 amperes
    B. 100 amperes
    C. 70 amperes
    D. 60 amperes

Again, the "question" is in the form of an incomplete statement and your task is to select the choice that best completes the statement. In this case, you are to find an exception. You have to select the MAXIMUM size circuit breaker the NEC® permits for overcurrent protection of the motor. You should have selected **A** because Section 430.6(A)(1) states, to determine the ampere rating of overcurrent protection for single-phase motors the FLC should be determined from Table 430.248, and Section 430.52(C)(1) Ex. 2(c) specifies the rating of an inverse time circuit breaker shall in no case exceed 400% of the full-load current of the motor.
FLC = 28 amperes x 400% = 112 amperes. Section 240.6(A) indicates a circuit breaker with a 110 ampere rating to be the next standard size with a lower value. If a circuit breaker of a higher value was selected, you would exceed 400% of the full-load current of the motor.

HOW TO USE THIS BOOK

Each "practice exam" contained in this book consists of twenty five questions. The time allotted for each "practice exam" is 90 minutes, 3.6 minutes per question. Using this time limit as a standard, you should be able to complete an actual examination in the allotted time. The "final exam" consists of one hundred questions; Journeyman need to get at least 70% of these questions correct; Masters should get at least 75% correct for a passing score.

To get the most out of this book, you should answer every question and highlight you NEC® for future reference. If you have difficulty with a question, skip it and come back to it after completing the remainder of the questions. Review your answers with the solutions at the back of the book. This will help you identify your strengths and weaknesses. When you discover you are weaker in some areas than others, you will know that further study is necessary in those areas.

Do only one or two "practice exams" contained in this book during an allotted study period; this way you do not get "burned out" and fatigued. This also helps you to develop good study habits.
GOOD LUCK!

ABOUT THE AUTHOR

H. Ray Holder of San Marcos, Texas, has worked in the electrical industry for over fifty years as an apprentice, journeyman, master, field engineer, estimator, business manager, contractor, consultant, inspector and instructor.

Mr. Holder is a graduate of Texas State University and holds a Bachelor of Science Degree in Occupational Education. He also holds a lifetime teaching certificate from the Texas Education Agency, in the field of Vocational Education.

He is a certified instructor of electrical trades. His classes are presented in a simplified, easy-to-understand format for electricians.

Since 1965 Mr. Holder has taught over 30,000 students at Austin Community College, and the University of Texas at Austin, Texas, Odessa College, at Odessa, Texas, Technical-Vocational Institute of Albuquerque, New Mexico, Howard College, at San Angelo, Texas and in the public school systems in Ft. Worth and San Antonio, Texas, as well as conducted electrical seminars throughout the United States. He is currently the Director of Education for Electrical Seminars, Inc. of San Marcos, Texas.

Mr. Holder is an active member of the National Fire Protection Association, International Association of Electrical Inspectors, and retired member of the International Brotherhood of Electrical Workers.

OTHER TITLES AVAILABLE BASED ON THE 2011 NEC®

Practical Calculations for Electricians

Electricians Exam Book

Electricians Handbook of NEC® Questions

USEFUL FORMULAS

To Find	Single Phase	Three Phase	Direct Current
Amperes when kVA is known	$\dfrac{kVA \times 1{,}000}{E}$	$\dfrac{kVA \times 1{,}000}{E \times 1.732}$	not applicable
Amperes when horsepower is known	$\dfrac{HP \times 746}{E \times \%Eff. \times PF.}$	$\dfrac{HP \times 746}{E \times 1.732 \times \%Eff. \times PF.}$	$\dfrac{HP \times 746}{E \times \%Eff.}$
Amperes when Kilowatts are known	$\dfrac{kW \times 1{,}000}{E \times PF.}$	$\dfrac{kW \times 1{,}000}{E \times 1.732 \times PF.}$	$\dfrac{kW \times 1{,}000}{E}$
Kilowatts	$\dfrac{I \times E \times PF.}{1{,}000}$	$\dfrac{I \times E \times 1.732 \times PF.}{1{,}000}$	$\dfrac{I \times E}{1{,}000}$
Kilovolt Amperes	$\dfrac{I \times E}{1{,}000}$	$\dfrac{I \times E \times 1.732}{1{,}000}$	not applicable
Horsepower	$\dfrac{I \times E \times \%Eff. \times PF.}{746}$	$\dfrac{I \times E \times 1.732 \times \%Eff. \times PF.}{746}$	$\dfrac{I \times E \times \%Eff.}{746}$
Watts	$E \times I \times PF.$	$E \times I \times 1.732 \times PF.$	$E \times I$

I = Amperes
E = Volt
kW = Kilowatts
kVA = Kilovolt-Amperes

HP = Horsepower
%Eff. = Percent Efficiency
PF. = Power Factor

Power – "Pie" Circle Formulas

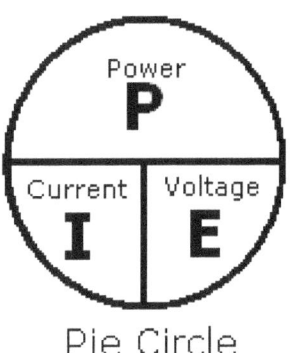
Pie Circle

I = P/E
To Find Current

P = I x E
To Find Power

E = P/I
To Find Voltage

Ohms Law Circle Formulas

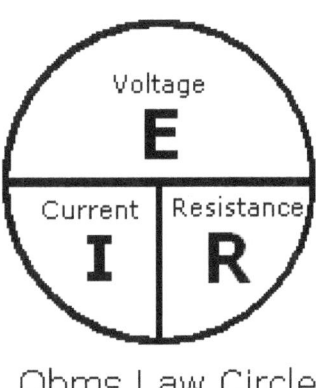
Ohms Law Circle

I = E/R
To Find Current

E = I x R
To Find Voltage

R = E/I
To Find Resistance

Copyright 2016   BrownTechnical.org

VOLTAGE DROP FORMULAS

Formula Definitions:

VD = Volts dropped from a circuit.

2 = Multiplying factor for single-phase circuits. The 2 represents the conductor length in a single-phase circuit.

1.732 = Multiplying factor for three-phase circuits. The square root of 3 represents the conductor length in a three-phase circuit. The only difference between the single-phase and three-phase formulas is that "1.732" has replaced "2".

K = Approximate resistivity of the conductor per mil foot. A mil foot is a wire 1 foot long and one mil in diameter. The approximate K value for copper wire is **12.9** ohms and for aluminum wire is **21.2** ohms per mil foot.

I = Current or amperage draw of the load.

D = The distance from the source voltage to the load.

CM = Circular mil area of the conductor. (Chapter 9, Table 8)

*NOTE – When determining wire size, distance or current, VD is the actual volts that can be dropped from the circuit. The recommended percentage for a branch-circuit is 3%. Example: 3% of 120 volts is 3.6 volts. DO NOT enter 3% in the VD position.

To find voltage drop in a single-phase circuit.

$$VD = \frac{2 \times K \times I \times D}{CM}$$

To find wire size in a single-phase circuit.

$$CM = \frac{2 \times K \times I \times D}{VD}$$

To find distance in a single-phase circuit.

$$D = \frac{CM \times VD}{2 \times K \times I}$$

To find MAXIMUM current in amperes in a single-phase circuit.

$$I = \frac{CM \times VD}{2 \times K \times D}$$

Power Factor Triangle Formulas

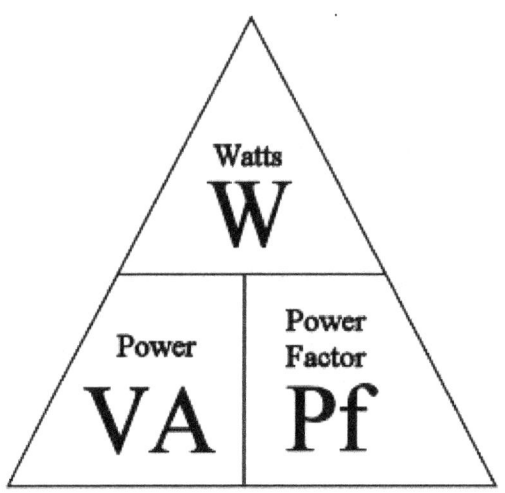

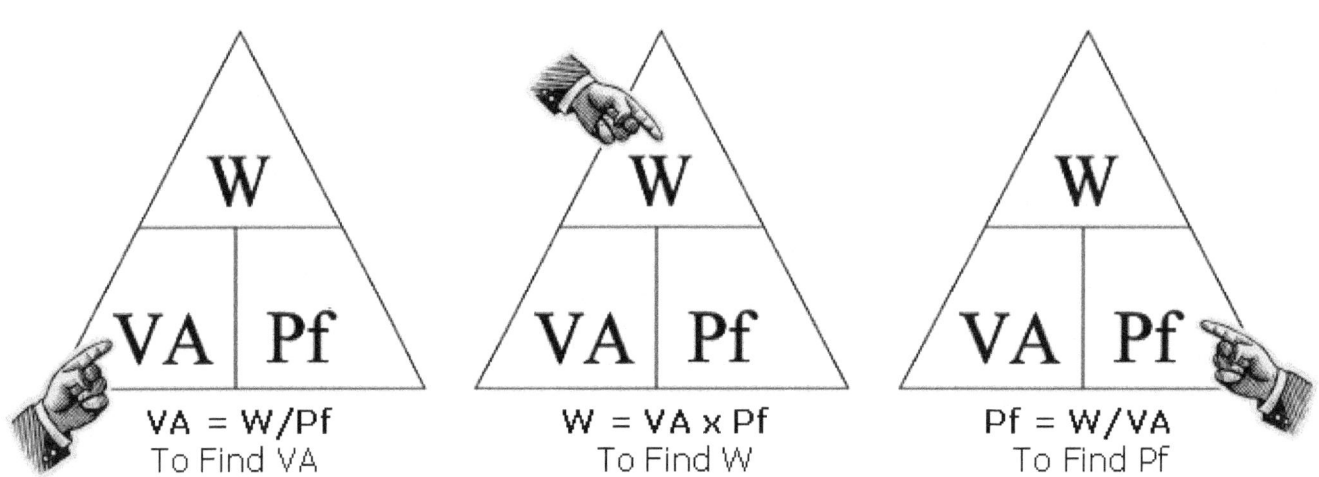

VA = W/Pf
To Find VA

W = VA x Pf
To Find W

Pf = W/VA
To Find Pf

ELECTRICIANS PRACTICE CALCULATIONS EXAMS
EXAM 1

These questions are typical of questions encountered on Journeyman Electricians' exams. This exam is based on the 2011 edition of the National Electrical Code®. The only material permitted for use on this type of exam is a calculator, scratch paper and a 2011 edition NEC® book. On each question select the best answer from the choices given and review your answers with the answer key included in this book.

ALLOTTED TIME: 90 minutes

1. A metal device box will contain the following:

   - 1 switch
   - 2 cable clamps
   - 1 bonding jumper
   - 2 spliced grounding conductors

   To allow for the grounding and bonding conductors, clamps and device, the maximum number of conductors permitted in the box must be REDUCED by _____ conductors.

   A. one
   B. two
   C. three
   D. four

2. When a 240-volt, single-phase branch-circuit has a current flow of 20 amperes, what is the resistance, in ohms, of this circuit?

   A. 3 ohms
   B. 6 ohms
   C. 9 ohms
   D. 12 ohms

3. Where a 1,500 watt residential baseboard heater is connected to a 240 volt, single-phase circuit, the current flow in this circuit is _____.

   A. 4.15 amperes
   B. 6.25 amperes
   C. 12.5 amperes
   D. 16.6 amperes

4. Determine the MAXIMUM allowable ampacity of a size 4 AWG copper conductor with type THWN insulation installed in a conduit 10 feet in length with five (5) other current-carrying conductors.

   A. 52 amperes
   B. 60 amperes
   C. 68 amperes
   D. 85 amperes

5. A 15 kW, 208-volt, single-phase heat pump will have a full-load current rating of _____.

   A. 72 amperes
   B. 46 amperes
   C. 66 amperes
   D. 33 amperes

6. Where a 150 kVA, single-phase transformer having a secondary voltage of 120/240 has been installed at a multifamily dwelling, the full-load current rating of the transformer secondary is _____.

   A. 329 amperes
   B. 421 amperes
   C. 625 amperes
   D. 729 amperes

7. Determine the MINIMUM number of 15-ampere, 120-volt, general lighting branch-circuits required for a one-family dwelling with 2,750 square feet of habitable space.

   A. three
   B. four
   C. five
   D. six

8. When a 120-volt branch-circuit has only six (6), 100 watt, 120 volt incandescent luminaires connected, what will be the measured current in the home run supplying this load?

    A. 30 amperes
    B. 20 amperes
    C. 5 amperes
    D. 1 ampere

9. Determine the MINIMUM ampacity required of the branch-circuit conductors supplying a Design B, 3-phase, 208-volt, 10 horsepower induction type motor used in a continuous-duty application.

    A. 30.8 amperes
    B. 46.2 amperes
    C. 38.5 amperes
    D. 32.2 amperes

10. Where a commercial building with a 3-phase, 208Y/120 volt, 4-wire service has a total load of 40 kVA after all demand factors have been taken into consideration, the MINIMUM size THW copper conductors required for the ungrounded service-entrance conductors are _____.

    A. 2 AWG
    B. 3 AWG
    C. 1/0 AWG
    D. 2/0 AWG

11. Determine the required volume, in cubic inches, for a junction box that will contain the following combination of conductors. Assume all conductors will carry current.

    - 4 – size 12 AWG with THHN insulation
    - 4 – size 10 AWG with THWN insulation
    - 4 – size 8 AWG with XHHW insulation

    A. 31.00 cubic inches
    B. 46.40 cubic inches
    C. 50.20 cubic inches
    D. 48.00 cubic inches

12. The MAXIMUM continuous load permitted for a lighting branch-circuit that is rated for 20-amperes is _____, because the circuit breaker protecting the circuit is NOT rated for continuous duty.

    A. 10 amperes
    B. 20 amperes
    C. 18 amperes
    D. 16 amperes

13. Where the input rating of a single-phase motor is 6,900 VA, what is the current flow in the conductors where the motor is rated for 230-volts?

    A. 15 amperes
    B. 30 amperes
    C. 60 amperes
    D. 80 amperes

14. Given: A hermetic refrigerant motor-compressor has a rated current of 20-amperes and a branch-circuit selection current rating of 26 amperes. The disconnecting means must be rated at LEAST _____.

    A. 20 amperes
    B. 23 amperes
    C. 26 amperes
    D. 30 amperes

15. Given: Three (3) size 1/0 AWG THW copper current-carrying conductors are to be contained within a common raceway. The ambient temperature will be 120 deg. F. Determine the allowable ampacity of the individual conductors.

    A. 113 amperes
    B. 130 amperes
    C. 146 amperes
    D. 150 amperes

16. How many 120-volt, 15-ampere rated branch-circuits are required for a 11,500 VA non-continuous lighting load?

    A. five
    B. six
    C. seven
    D. eight

17. A one-family dwelling to be constructed will have an air-conditioning load of 7,200 VA. The house will also have an electrical central heating unit rated at 15 kVA. Where applying the optional method of calculations for dwellings, a MINIMUM total VA load of _____ is to be added to the service load calculation for the AC and/or heating loads.

    A. 15,000 VA
    B. 9,750 VA
    C. 14,430 VA
    D. 18,750 VA

18. Where a microwave oven is rated at 1,200 watts, how much current will the oven draw when connected to a 120-volt, single-phase, branch-circuit?

    A. .1 ampere
    B. 5 amperes
    C. 10 amperes
    D. 15 amperes

19. What is the MAXIMUM demand load, in VA, that may be connected to a 150-ampere rated 120/240 volt, single-phase residential service?

    A. 180,000 VA
    B. 90,000 VA
    C. 36,000 VA
    D. 72,000 VA

20. Apply the general method of calculation for dwellings, and determine the demand load, in kW, on the ungrounded service-entrance conductors for an 8.5 kW electric range.

    A. 6.8 kW
    B. 8.0 kW
    C. 8.5 kW
    D. 10.6 kW

21. What is the ampacity of a size 10 AWG THW copper conductor, when four (4) conductors of the same size and insulation are contained in a conduit 25 feet long? Given: All conductors are current-carrying and the ambient temperature is 50 deg. C.

    A. 30 amperes
    B. 28 amperes
    C. 26 amperes
    D. 21 amperes

22. As per the NEC®, what is the recommended MAXIMUM voltage drop for a 120-volt lighting branch-circuit?

    A. 1 volt
    B. 2 volts
    C. 3.6 volts
    D. 6 volts

23. Given: A 45 ampere, 240-volt, single-phase load is located 175 feet from a panelboard and is supplied with size 6 AWG THWN copper branch-circuit conductors. Determine the approximate voltage drop on the conductors. (K=12.9)

    A. 6.70 volts
    B. 7.74 volts
    C. 3.20 volts
    D. 9.60 volts

24. What is the MAXIMUM continuous-load, in VA, that a 240-volt, single-phase branch-circuit may be protected with a 20-ampere rated circuit breaker not rated for continuous use?

    A. 2,400 VA
    B. 2,850 VA
    C. 3,840 VA
    D. 4,800 VA

25. Determine what MINIMUM size THWN copper conductors are required to supply a continuous-duty, 25 hp, 3-phase, 208-volt, Design B motor. Assume all terminations are rated for 75 deg. C.

    A. 1 AWG
    B. 2 AWG
    C. 3 AWG
    D. 4 AWG

END OF EXAM 1

ELECTRICIANS PRACTICE CALCULATIONS EXAMS
EXAM 2

These questions are typical of questions encountered on Journeyman Electricians' exams. This exam is based on the 2011 edition of the National Electrical Code®. The only material permitted for use on this type of exam is a calculator, scratch paper and a 2011 edition NEC® book. On each question select the best answer from the choices given and review your answers with the answer key included in this book.

ALLOTTED TIME: 90 minutes

1. Determine the power consumed, in VA, by a lighting load which operates at 115 volts, draws 8 amperes, and has a power factor of 80 percent.

    A. 1,150 VA
    B. 960 VA
    C. 920 VA
    D. 736 VA

2. Given: A trade size 2 in. rigid metal conduit (RMC) to be installed will contain four (4) size 3/0 AWG THWN copper conductors. The conduit is to be bent with a full shoe bending machine. What is the MINIMUM bend radius of the conduit?

    A. 9½ inches
    B. 12 inches
    C. 15 inches
    D. 19 inches

3. When conduit nipples having a MAXIMUM length NOT to exceed _____ are installed between boxes and similar enclosures, the nipples shall be permitted to be filled to 60 percent of their cross-sectional area.

    A. 6 inches
    B. 12 inches
    C. 18 inches
    D. 24 inches

4. Determine the largest trade size raceway permitted to be installed in a junction box, where given the following related information:

    - junction box is 12 inches in length
    - conductors are size 4 AWG
    - a straight pull of the conductors is to be made

    A. 1 inch
    B. 1¼ inches
    C. 1½ inches
    D. 2 inches

Questions 5 through 10 are based on the following related information given for a retail store building with dimensions of 100 feet x 75 feet.

- Service is 120/240 volts, 3-wire, single-phase.
- Actual connected lighting load of 14,000 VA.
- The building has 50 feet of show window lighting.
- The store has a total of 115 general-use 125-volt duplex receptacles.
- Consider all the overcurrent protection devices NOT to be listed for continuous use.

5. When calculating the total load of the building, what MINIMUM load, in VA, must be included for the general-use duplex receptacles?

    A. 11,500 VA
    B. 15,350 VA
    C. 16,560 VA
    D. 20,700 VA

6. Determine the MINIMUM number of 20-ampere, 120-volt, branch-circuits required for the general-use duplex receptacles.

    A. nine
    B. eight
    C. seven
    D. six

7. When calculating the total load on the building, what MINIMUM VA must be included for the general lighting load? Consider the main circuit breaker NOT to be listed for continuous use.

    A. 14,000 VA
    B. 18,000 VA
    C. 22,500 VA
    D. 28,125 VA

8. Determine the MINIMUM number of 20-ampere, 120-volt branch-circuits required for the general lighting load of the retail store building. Circuit breakers of this size are NOT rated for continuous use.

    A. six
    B. twelve
    C. ten
    D. eight

9. When calculating the total load on the retail store, what MINIMUM load, in VA, must be included for the show window lighting?

    A. 9,000 VA
    B. 10,000 VA
    C. 11,250 VA
    D. 12,500 VA

10. After demand factors are taken into consideration, when calculating the total load on the above referenced building, what MINIMUM VA must be included for the combined loads of the general lighting, general-use receptacles and the show window lighting?

    A. 55,975 VA
    B. 61,325 VA
    C. 44,100 VA
    D. 48,200 VA

11. Determine the voltage drop on a branch-circuit given the following related information:

    - current = 5 amperes
    - conductor length = 300 feet
    - conductor resistance = 4 ohms/1000 ft.

    A. 0.02 volts
    B. 0.12 volts
    C. 1.20 volts
    D. 6 volts

12. For the purposes of determining conductor fill in conduit, what is the total area, in square inches, of three (3) size 4/0 AWG THWN and three (3) size 2/0 AWG THWN conductors?

    A. 1.174 square inches
    B. 1.638 square inches
    C. 2.048 square inches
    D. 3.522 square inches

13. If two (2) conductors in a 120-volt circuit are shorted together, and the conductors each have a resistance of .004 ohms, what is the MAXIMUM short circuit current possible?

    A. 0.48 amperes
    B. 20 amperes
    C. 15,000 amperes
    D. 60,000 amperes

14. Given: The following listed electrical equipment is to be installed in a restaurant that has a 120/240 volt, 3-wire, single-phase service.

    - One – 240-volt, 5 kVA booster heater
    - One – 240-volt, 3.5 kVA cooktop
    - One – 240-volt, 9 kVA oven

    After taking demand factors into consideration, what load, in amperes, would this equipment add to the ungrounded (line) service-entrance conductors?

    A. 45 amperes
    B. 58 amperes
    C. 73 amperes
    D. 66 amperes

15. A 15 kVA, 240-volt, single-phase generator is capable of supplying a MAXIMUM load of _____.

    A. 16 amperes
    B. 36 amperes
    C. 63 amperes
    D. 76 amperes

16. Where there is no secondary overcurrent protection provided, determine the MAXIMUM size fuses required to protect the primary of a 480-volt, single-phase, 20 kVA transformer.

    A. 45 amperes
    B. 50 amperes
    C. 60 amperes
    D. 70 amperes

17. Determine the amperage draw of a 10 hp, single-phase, 208-volt motor that operates at 90 percent efficiency, with 85 percent power factor.

    A. 46.88 amperes
    B. 50.00 amperes
    C. 28.08 amperes
    D. 61.10 amperes

18. How much expansion can be expected in a rigid polyvinyl chloride conduit (PVC) that is 250 feet long and is installed in an environment that is subject to a 100° F temperature change annually?

    A. 4.06 inches
    B. 6.08 inches
    C. 8.16 inches
    D. 10.15 inches

19. Given: A fifty (50) foot long electrical metallic tubing (EMT) to be installed will contain the following insulated conductors.

    - four – size 12 AWG THHN
    - three – size 6 AWG THW
    - three – size 4 AWG THW
    - three – size 2 AWG THW

    Determine the MINIMUM trade size EMT the NEC® requires for this installation.

    A. 1½ in.
    B. 1¼ in.
    C. 2 in.
    D. 2½ in.

20. What is the full-load current of a 5 hp, 240-volt, single-phase, ac motor with a 75 percent efficiency rating?

    A. 21 amperes
    B. 12 amperes
    C. 16 amperes
    D. 28 amperes

21. Given: A rigid metal conduit (RMC) will contain only the following three (3) circuits:
    - two – 150 ampere, 3-phase circuits
    - one – 300 ampere, single-phase circuit

    The load side equipment bonding jumper for this circuit must be a MINIMUM size of _____ copper.

    A. 1 AWG
    B. 2 AWG
    C. 4 AWG
    D. 6 AWG

22. A feeder supplying two (2) continuous-duty, induction type, Design B, 208-volt, three-phase motors, one 10 hp and one 7½ hp, shall have a MINIMUM ampacity of _____.

    A. 55.00 amperes
    B. 68.75 amperes
    C. 62.70 amperes
    D. 38.50 amperes

23. Determine the MAXIMUM number of 120-volt, general-use receptacles the NEC® permits to be protected by a 20-ampere, 120-volt, single-phase circuit breaker when located in a commercial building.

    A. eighteen
    B. fifteen
    C. thirteen
    D. ten

24. The MINIMUM size device box required for six (6) size 12 AWG THHN conductors, and one (1) three-way switch is _____. Consider the box to have two (2) internal clamps.

    A. 12 cubic inches
    B. 18 cubic inches
    C. 15 cubic inches
    D. 21 cubic inches

25. Given: A commercial building has a 208Y/120 volt, 3-phase, 4-wire service with a balanced load of 12 kVA per phase; 36 kVA total load. Determine the load, in amperes on the ungrounded (phase) service-entrance conductors.

   A. 100 amperes
   B. 200 amperes
   C. 300 amperes
   D. 33.3 amperes

END OF EXAM 2

ELECTRICIANS PRACTICE CALCULATIONS EXAMS
EXAM 3

These questions are typical of questions encountered on Journeyman Electricians' exams. This exam is based on the 2011 edition of the National Electrical Code®. The only material permitted for use on this type of exam is a calculator, scratch paper and a 2011 edition NEC® book. On each question select the best answer from the choices given and review your answers with the answer key included in this book.

ALLOTTED TIME: 90 minutes

1. Using the general (standard) method of calculation on a one-family dwelling, determine the MINIMUM demand load, in VA, on the ungrounded (line) service-entrance conductors when the house has the following fixed appliances:

   - water heater — 4,800 VA
   - dishwasher — 1,200 VA
   - garbage disposal — 1,150 VA
   - trash compactor — 800 VA
   - attic fan — 1,200 VA

   A. 6,863 VA
   B. 9,150 VA
   C. 8,579 VA
   D. 11,438 VA

2. For dwelling units, the feeder and service neutral (grounded conductor) demand load for electric clothes dryers shall be calculated at a MINIMUM of _____ of the demand load on the ungrounded (line) conductors as determined by Table 220.54

   A. 100 percent
   B. 75 percent
   C. 80 percent
   D. 70 percent

3. A one-family dwelling unit with a 120/240 volt, single-phase service has a demand load of 36,000 VA. Determine the MINIMUM size ungrounded service-entrance conductors the NEC® permits, where installing aluminum conductors with THWN insulation.

    A. 1 AWG
    B. 1/0 AWG
    C. 2/0 AWG
    D. 3/0 AWG

4. The power factor of a 5 kW load drawing 30 amperes when connected to a 208-volt, single-phase source is _____.

    A. 92 percent
    B. 46 percent
    C. 80 percent
    D. 83 percent

5. Given: A commercial building has a total non-continuous load of 12,200 VA and a total continuous load of 16,200 VA. Determine the MINIMUM size standard fuses permitted to be used for overcurrent protection on the disconnecting means. The service is 120/240 volts, single-phase.

    A. 110 ampere
    B. 135 ampere
    C. 200 ampere
    D. 150 ampere

6. What is the electric dryer demand load, in watts, on the ungrounded (line) service-entrance conductors for a six (6) unit multifamily dwelling with a 5.5 kW dryer in each unit? (Apply the general method of calculations for dwelling units).

    A. 33,000 watts
    B. 21,000 watts
    C. 24,750 watts
    D. 26,400 watts

7. Determine the MAXIMUM number of size 4/0 AWG, three-wire, multi-conductor cables rated at 600 volts, the NEC® permits to be installed in a 24 inch wide solid bottom cable tray. Assume a three-conductor, 4/0 AWG cable has an outside dimension of 1½ inches.

    A. fourteen
    B. thirteen
    C. sixteen
    D. fifteen

8. Given: A transformer arc welder has a duty-cycle of 60 percent and a primary current of 40 amperes. The ampacity of the branch-circuit conductors supplying this welder must be at LEAST _____.

    A. 24 amperes
    B. 40 amperes
    C. 31 amperes
    D. 50 amperes

9. The overcurrent protection to be provided for the arc welder referenced in the above question is to be rated at NO more than _____.

    A. 40 amperes
    B. 50 amperes
    C. 75 amperes
    D. 80 amperes

10. Determine the branch-circuit load, in amperes, for a 120-volt branch circuit in a commercial building that supplies ten (10) general-use duplex receptacles and six (6) 100 watt luminaires. Consider the loads to be noncontinuous.

    A. 5 amperes
    B. 10 amperes
    C. 20 amperes
    D. 25 amperes

11. What is the MAXIMUM number of size 4/0 AWG copper conductors with XHHW insulation the NEC® permits to be installed in a trade size 3 in. intermediate metal conduit (IMC) where the conduit is only 19 inches long?

    A. nine
    B. thirteen
    C. fourteen
    D. fifteen

12. What is the MINIMUM size copper conductors for a 120-volt branch circuit the NEC® permits where the load is 100 feet from the panelboard, the K value is 12.9, circuit current is 16 amperes and the voltage drop is limited to 3 percent?

    A. 6 AWG
    B. 8 AWG
    C. 10 AWG
    D. 12 AWG

13. Determine the allowable ampacity of a copper size 12/2 AWG with ground Type NM cable when the cable is bundled together for six (6) feet with three (3) other 120-volt branch-circuits using the same cable.

    A. 17.5 amperes
    B. 20 amperes
    C. 21 amperes
    D. 25 amperes

14. Determine the MAXIMUM size inverse time circuit breaker for branch-circuit, short-circuit and ground-fault protection the NEC® permits for a 10 hp, 208-volt, 3-phase, Design B, continuous-duty, squirrel cage motor. Assume no exceptions are applicable.

    A. 35 amperes
    B. 70 amperes
    C. 75 amperes
    D. 80 amperes

15. Given: A commercial building has a 208Y/120 volt, 3-phase, 4-wire electrical system. After taking demand factors into consideration, the loads on the ungrounded (phase) conductors at a sub-panel are as follows:

    - Phase A – 7,200 VA
    - Phase B – 8,400 VA
    - Phase C – 9,600 VA

    Determine the current on phase B.

    A. 70 amperes
    B. 23 amperes
    C. 40 amperes
    D. 60 amperes

16. When a 20-ampere, 120-volt load is located 150 feet from a panelboard and is supplied with size 10 AWG THWN-2 copper conductors, what is the approximate voltage drop on the branch-circuit conductors?   (K = 12.9)

    A. 1.8 volts
    B. 9.5 volts
    C. 7.5 volts
    D. 15 volts

17. What is the percentage of voltage drop on the above referenced question?

    A. 3 percent
    B. 5 percent
    C. 6.2 percent
    D. 5.8 percent

18. How many size 12 AWG THWN-2 conductors may be installed in a 3½ inch deep, 3-gang masonry box that contains three (3) switches?

    A. twenty-one
    B. twenty-three
    C. twenty-four
    D. twenty-seven

19. What is the MAXIMUM load, in VA, permitted for a 208Y/120 volt, three-phase, 4-wire, 150-ampere service?

    A. 18,000 VA
    B. 31,200 VA
    C. 54,038 VA
    D. 93,600 VA

20. What MINIMUM trade size rigid metal conduit (RMC) nipple, 20 inches long, is required by the NEC® to enclose three (3) size 3/0 AWG THWN conductors, one (1) size 1 AWG THWN and one (1) size 6 AWG THWN conductor?

    A. 2 in.
    B. 1¼ in.
    C. 1½ in.
    D. none of these

21. What is the calculated current through conductors supplying a 3.5 kW water heater operating at 240-volts, single-phase?

    A. 0.014 amperes
    B. 14.6 amperes
    C. 68 amperes
    D. 84 amperes

22. Given: A conduit is installed in an equipment room of a commercial building having an ambient temperature of 97 deg. F. The conduit will contain one (1) size 4/0 AWG THWN grounded conductor and two (2) size 4/0 AWG THWN ungrounded conductors. What is the allowable ampacity of the ungrounded conductors as permitted by the NEC®? All conductors are assumed to be copper.

    A. 164 amperes
    B. 197 amperes
    C. 202 amperes
    D. 230 amperes

23. Given: A one-family dwelling has three (3) small appliance branch circuits and a laundry branch-circuit. Before demand factors are taken into consideration, the total computed load, in VA, on these branch circuits is _____.

    A. 1,500 VA
    B. 3,000 VA
    C. 4,500 VA
    D. 6,000 VA

24. Determine the MINIMUM size Type NM cable the NEC® requires for branch-circuit conductors, supplying a 10 kW, 240-volt, single-phase, residential electric range.

    A. 10 AWG
    B. 8 AWG
    C. 6 AWG
    D. 4 AWG

25. Given: A 500-ampere rated commercial building service is supplied by two (2) parallel size 350 kcmil aluminum conductors per phase. What is the MINIMUM size copper grounding electrode conductor required where connected to the concrete-encased building reinforcement bars used as the grounding electrode?

    A. 2 AWG
    B. 1/0 AWG
    C. 2/0 AWG
    D. 3/0 AWG

END OF EXAM 3

ELECTRICIANS PRACTICE CALCULATIONS EXAMS
EXAM 4

These questions are typical of questions encountered on Journeyman Electricians' exams. This exam is based on the 2011 edition of the National Electrical Code®. The only material permitted for use on this type of exam is a calculator, scratch paper and a 2011 edition NEC® book. On each question select the best answer from the choices given and review your answers with the answer key included in this book.

ALLOTTED TIME: 90 minutes

1. Determine the MINIMUM size THWN copper conductors the NEC® requires to serve a 15 minute rated short-time duty motor, with a nameplate ampere rating of 25 amperes. The terminations are rated for 75 deg. C.

    A. 12 AWG
    B. 10 AWG
    C. 8 AWG
    D. 6 AWG

2. Given: A 15-ampere rated ac general-use snap switch is to serve as a disconnecting means for a motor of 2 hp or less and rated 240-volts. The NEC® requires the MAXIMUM full-load current rating of the motor to be no more than _____.

    A. 7.5 amperes
    B. 10 amperes
    C. 12 amperes
    D. 15 amperes

3. What is the total resistance of a series circuit with resistors that have values of 2 ohms, 4 ohms, 6 ohms and 10 ohms?

    A. 0.98 ohms
    B. 1.01 ohms
    C. 22 ohms
    D. 20 ohms

4. If the previous referenced series circuit is served with a 240-volt, single-phase power source, what would be the total current?

    A. 10.9 amperes
    B. 21.8 amperes
    C. 0.09 amperes
    D. 1.01 amperes

5. Determine the MAXIMUM line current, in amperes, on a balanced 3-phase, 4-wire, system with a MAXIMUM load per phase of 25 kVA and a line voltage of 208Y/120 volts. Total power is 75 kVA.

    A. 87 amperes
    B. 144 amperes
    C. 208 amperes
    D. 360 amperes

6. How many square inches of ventilation is required for a transformer vault ventilated by natural circulation of air to an outdoor area, where the vault houses a 150 kVA, 3-phase transformer?

    A. 50 square inches
    B. 150 square inches
    C. 450 square inches
    D. 750 square inches

7. How many 300 watt industrial type lighting fixtures may be installed on a branch-circuit rated at 20-amperes, 120-volts? Assume the luminaires operate eight (8) continuous hours and the overcurrent device for the circuit is not approved for continuous duty.

    A. four
    B. five
    C. six
    D. seven

8. Determine the cross-sectional area, in square inches, for the following combination of conductors:

   - two – size 14 AWG THW
   - ten – size 10 AWG RHW without outer covering

   A. 0.3608 square inches
   B. 0.3940 square inches
   C. 0.4480 square inches
   D. 0.5010 square inches

9. Given: A flexible metal conduit (FMC) to be installed will contain three (3) size 400 kcmil THWN copper conductors and one (1) size 250 kcmil THWN copper conductor. What MINIMUM trade size FMC is permitted for this installation?

   A. 3 in.
   B. 3½ in.
   C. 4 in.
   D. 2½ in.

10. Determine the MAXIMUM number of size 1/0 AWG THWN-2 copper conductors the NEC® permits to be installed in a 4 inch x 4 inch metal wireway.

    A. seventeen
    B. eighteen
    C. twenty
    D. thirty

11. A branch-circuit supplying a fixed storage-type water heater, rated 9 kW at 240-volts, single-phase, is required to have a MINIMUM ampacity of _____.

    A. 37.50 amperes
    B. 56.00 amperes
    C. 46.90 amperes
    D. 13.45 amperes

12. A 3-phase, 240-volt, 7½ hp, Design C, 50 deg. C rise motor has a FLA of 20-amperes indicated on the nameplate. The MINIMUM rating of the overload device used to protect this motor as required by the NEC® is _____.

    A. 20 amperes
    B. 23 amperes
    C. 25 amperes
    D. 26 amperes

13. Refer to the previous question. Assume the MINIMUM rating of the overload device you have selected will not allow the motor to start without tripping. Determine the MAXIMUM overload device, in amperes, the NEC® permits to be used to protect this motor.

    A. 23 amperes
    B. 25 amperes
    C. 28 amperes
    D. 26 amperes

14. What is the rated secondary current of a 600 VA, single-phase transformer at unity power factor, which has a 200 volt input and a 15 volt secondary?

    A. 10 amperes
    B. 20 amperes
    C. 13 amperes
    D. 40 amperes

15. Where a recreational vehicle park has 200 sites with electrical power supplied, how many RV sites are required to have a 30-ampere, 125 volt receptacle provided at the site?

    A. two-hundred
    B. one-hundred and forty
    C. one-hundred
    D. ten

16. A trade size 2 inch raceway is to be installed in a pull box for a straight pull; conductors are size 1/0 AWG THWN. What is the MINIMUM length of the pull box as required by the NEC®?

    A. 4 inches
    B. 12 inches
    C. 16 inches
    D. 24 inches

17. A device box to be installed will contain four (4) size 10 AWG conductors and four (4) size 12 AWG conductors. Assuming each conductor carries current, for the purposes of determining box fill, these conductors are equivalent to _____.

    A. 20 cubic inches
    B. 19 cubic inches
    C. 18 cubic inches
    D. 17 cubic inches

18. A one-family dwelling is to be supplied with a 120/240 volt service drop from the local utility company. After all demand factors have been taken into consideration, there is a calculated demand load of 48 kW. Determine the MINIMUM size THWN aluminum ungrounded service-entrance conductors as required by the NEC®.

    A. 2/0 AWG
    B. 3/0 AWG
    C. 4/0 AWG
    D. 250 kcmil

19. A 5 hp single-phase, 208-volt, continuous-duty, induction-type motor has a nameplate current rating of 25 amperes. Disregarding exceptions, what is the MINIMUM size type THW copper conductors that may be used to supply this motor? Assume all terminations are rated 75º.

    A. 6 AWG
    B. 8 AWG
    C. 10 AWG
    D. 12 AWG

20. A twenty-five (25) unit mobile home park is to be built, and the mobile homes occupying the spaces are calculated at a demand of 15,000 VA each. For the purpose of calculating the service load, determine the MINIMUM allowable demand load, in VA, the NEC® permits on the ungrounded service-entrance conductors for the mobile home park.

    A. 400,000 VA
    B. 375,000 VA
    C. 90,000 VA
    D. 96,000 VA

21. Refer to the above question. Where the mobile home park is supplied with a 120/240 volt, 3-wire, single-phase service, this requires a MINIMUM size service of _____.

    A. 1,667 amperes
    B. 1,563 amperes
    C. 400 amperes
    D. 375 amperes

22. All of the following copper conductors are to be installed in an electrical metallic tubing (EMT) that is fifty (50) feet long.

    - 24 – size 10 AWG TW
    - 10 – size 10 AWG THW
    - 14 – size 12 AWG THHN

    Determine the MINIMUM standard trade size of EMT required.

    A. 2 in.
    B. 2½ in.
    C. 3 in.
    D. 3½ in.

23. The absolute MAXIMUM rating of an inverse time circuit breaker for branch-circuit, short-circuit and ground-fault protection allowed for a 40 hp, 230-volt, 3-phase, continuous-duty motor is _____.

    A. 150 amperes
    B. 200 amperes
    C. 250 amperes
    D. 300 amperes

24. Where an apartment complex has a lighting load of 205.4 kVA, determine the lighting demand load, in kVA. Each apartment contains an electric range. (The optional method is not to be used.)

    A. 58.9 kVA
    B. 60.2 kVA
    C. 16.5 kVA
    D. 65.3 kVA

25. A 10,800 VA, 240-volt, single-phase load is located 200 feet from a panelboard and is supplied with size 6 AWG THWN-2 copper conductors. Determine the approximate voltage drop on the conductors. (K = 12.9)

    A. 8.84 volts
    B. 7.72 volts
    C. 3.26 volts
    D. 9.67 volts

END OF EXAM 4

ELECTRICIANS PRACTICE CALCULATIONS EXAMS
EXAM 5

These questions are typical of questions encountered on Journeyman Electricians' exams. This exam is based on the 2011 edition of the National Electrical Code®. The only material permitted for use on this type of exam is a calculator, scratch paper and a 2011 edition NEC® book. On each question select the best answer from the choices given and review your answers with the answer key included in this book.

ALLOTTED TIME: 90 minutes

1. Where an electrical conduit is installed outdoors three (3) inches above a rooftop and exposed to direct sunlight, for the purpose of determining the allowable ampacity of the conductors contained within the raceway, a temperature value of _____ is required to be added to the anticipated ambient temperature.

    A. 60° F
    B. 40° F
    C. 30° F
    D. 25° F

2. Determine the total resistance of 375 feet of a size 10 AWG THW stranded copper conductor when used under normal conditions.

    A. 1.24 ohms
    B. 0.0124 ohms
    C. 0.00124 ohms
    D. 0.456 ohms

3. Determine the MAXIMUM size circuit breaker that may be used to protect a 30 gallon residential water heater, given the following:

    - water heater is rated 3,600 VA at 240-volts.
    - conductors supplying the water heater are size 8 AWG NM cable.

    A. 20 amperes
    B. 25 amperes
    C. 30 amperes
    D. 50 amperes

4. The MINIMUM number of 120-volt, 15-ampere general-purpose lighting and receptacle branch-circuits required for a dwelling that has 70 feet by 30 feet of livable space is _____.

    A. two
    B. three
    C. four
    D. five

5. When using the general method of load calculation for a one-family dwelling, what is the service demand load, in kW, on the ungrounded service-entrance conductors for one (1) 18 kW rated residential electric range?

    A. 12.0 KW
    B. 10.4 KW
    C. 8.0 KW
    D. 18 KW

6. Determine the conductor ampacity given the following related information:

    - Conductors are size 12 AWG THHN copper.
    - Ambient temperature is 108 deg. F.
    - Three (3) current-carrying conductors are in the raceway.
    - Raceway is 40 feet in length.

    A. 26.1 amperes
    B. 21.75 amperes
    C. 30.0 amperes
    D. 17.4 amperes

7. What is the MINIMUM demand load, in VA, for the general-purpose receptacles when an office building has seventy-five (75) general-purpose duplex receptacles located within the building?

    A. 11,750 VA
    B. 10,000 VA
    C. 18,500 VA
    D. 13,500 VA

8. A 15 foot intermediate metal conduit (IMC) to be installed will contain the following copper conductors:

    - Three – size 250 kcmil THWN
    - One – size 2 AWG bare

    What is the MINIMUM allowable trade size of IMC raceway as permitted by the NEC®?

    A. 1¼ in.
    B. 1½ in.
    C. 2 in.
    D. 2½ in.

9. If a single-phase electric range rated at 53 amperes at 240-volts is operated on 208-volts, how much power does it consume?

    A. 1.70 kVA
    B. 9.55 kVA
    C. 11.0 kVA
    D. 12.7 kVA

10. For a junction box, how many cubic inches of volume shall be allowed for each size 4 AWG conductor housed in the box?

    A. 6 cubic inches
    B. 3 cubic inches
    C. 5 cubic inches
    D. None of these

11. You are to supply a 240-volt, single-phase, 3-wire, 200-ampere, non-continuous load in an area where the expected ambient temperature is 120 deg. F. Using THWN copper conductors, determine the MINIMUM size as required by the NEC®.

    A. 300 kcmil
    B. 250 kcmil
    C. 4/0 AWG
    D. 3/0 AWG

12. Where a motor-generator arc welder has a 75 ampere rated primary current and a 90 percent duty cycle, determine the MAXIMUM standard size circuit breaker the NEC® permits for overcurrent protection for this welder.

    A. 100 amperes
    B. 125 amperes
    C. 150 amperes
    D. 200 amperes

13. What is the MINIMUM length required of a junction box used in a straight run of 1½ inch rigid metal conduit (RMC) containing three (3) size 1 AWG THWN conductors?

    A. 6 inches
    B. 8 inches
    C. 10 inches
    D. 12 inches

14. How many 120-volt, 20-ampere, branch-circuits are required for 200 feet of track lighting installed in a retail store? Given: The luminaires are on continuously for eight (8) hours or more and circuit breakers of this size are not rated for continuous use.

    A. eight
    B. seven
    C. six
    D. four

15. According to the NEC® tables, what is the full-load running current of a 30 hp, 230-volt, 3-phase synchronous motor with a 90 percent power factor?

    A. 63.0 amperes
    B. 69.3 amperes
    C. 76.23 amperes
    D. 86.62 amperes

16. Determine the circuit resistance, in ohms, when 1,000 watts is connected to a source voltage of 240-volts.

    A. 4.17 ohms
    B. 57.7 ohms
    C. 64.0 ohms
    D. 6,760 ohms

17. A controller (contactor) is to be installed to control an automatically started 1 hp ac motor with a marked service factor of 1.15. The motor nameplate full-load current rating is 8.8 amperes. What is the MAXIMUM size overload device that may be installed in this controller?

   A. 10.1 amperes
   B. 11.0 amperes
   C. 11.8 amperes
   D. 12.3 amperes

18. When calculating the total load for a farm service, what is the MINIMUM service size, using the standard size of overcurrent devices, for a farm service when five (5) 60 ampere loads are installed in the main panelboard?

   A. 200 amperes
   B. 225 amperes
   C. 250 amperes
   D. 300 amperes

19. What is the MINIMUM number of 30-ampere, 240-volt branch-circuits required for 24 baseboard heaters, each rated at 1,750 watts @ 240 volts?

   A. six
   B. eight
   C. ten
   D. twelve

20. Determine the MINIMUM size NM cable the NEC® permits for branch circuit conductors serving a 10 kW, 240-volt, wall-mounted oven in a dwelling.

   A. 6 AWG
   B. 8 AWG
   C. 10 AWG
   D. 12 AWG

21. If a 240-volt resistance heater is connected to a 208 voltage source, what percentage of its rated power will it consume?

   A. 65 percent
   B. 70 percent
   C. 75 percent
   D. 87 percent

22. Determine the demand, in VA, on the ungrounded (line) service-entrance conductors for a 30-ampere, 240-volt, single-phase electric clothes dryer with using the standard method of calculation for a one-family dwelling.

    A. 5,000 VA
    B. 5,040 VA
    C. 7,200 VA
    D. 3,500 VA

23. When using non-time delay fuses, which one of the fuses listed below is the MAXIMUM size the NEC® permits for short-circuit and ground-fault protection for a 3/4 hp, single-phase, 240-volt pump motor? Disregard exceptions.

    A. 10 amperes
    B. 15 amperes
    C. 20 amperes
    D. 30 amperes

24. Determine the MINIMUM size copper NMC cable the NEC® requires for branch circuit conductors to supply a single-phase, 240-volt, 17 kW residential electric range.

    A. 8 AWG
    B. 6 AWG
    C. 4 AWG
    D. 2 AWG

25. Determine the general lighting and general-use receptacle demand load, in VA, for the guest rooms of a twenty-four (24) unit motel. Each guest room has 600 square feet of living area.

    A. 14,400 VA
    B. 13,520 VA
    C. 21,600 VA
    D. 28,800 VA

END OF EXAM 5

ELECTRICIANS PRACTICE CALCULATIONS EXAMS
EXAM 6

These questions are typical of questions encountered on Journeyman Electricians' exams. This exam is based on the 2011 edition of the National Electrical Code®. The only material permitted for use on this type of exam is a calculator, scratch paper and a 2011 edition NEC® book. On each question select the best answer from the choices given and review your answers with the answer key included in this book.

ALLOTTED TIME: 90 minutes

1. Given: A single-resistance type seam welder is rated 50-amperes, primary current at 240-volts, with a 50 percent duty cycle. The circuit breaker protecting the welder is rated 60°C. What is the MINIMUM size THHN copper branch-circuit conductors the NEC® permits to supply the welder?

    A. 10 AWG
    B. 8 AWG
    C. 6 AWG
    D. 4 AWG

2. Determine the MAXIMUM size time-delay fuses the NEC® permits for overcurrent protection of a 240-volt, single-phase, 42 ampere, hermetic refrigerant motor-compressor.

    A. 70 amperes
    B. 80 amperes
    C. 85 amperes
    D. 90 amperes

3. The MINIMUM standard size ampere rating permitted for a circuit breaker protecting a residential central electric heating unit rated 18 kW, 240-volts, single-phase is _____.

    A. 75 amperes
    B. 80 amperes
    C. 90 amperes
    D. 100 amperes

4. What is the MINIMUM receptacle load, in VA, for forty-two (42) general-purpose duplex receptacles installed in an office building?

   A. 4,200 VA
   B. 7,560 VA
   C. 9,450 VA
   D. 5,250 VA

5. Given: A 3 in. x 2 in. x 3½ in. metal device box with internal NM clamps will contain a receptacle outlet supplied with a size 14/2 with ground NM cable. How many additional insulated size 14 AWG conductors are allowed to be installed in the box?

   A. two
   B. three
   C. four
   D. five

6. Given: A mobile home park has twenty-six (26) mobile homes each with a computed load of 22,000 VA. What is the MINIMUM ampacity required for the ungrounded service-entrance conductors serving this park?

   A. 260 amperes
   B. 572 amperes
   C. 1,000 amperes
   D. 1,750 amperes

7. Determine the MINIMUM required ampacity of the conductors supplying an elevator motor given the following:

   - 5 hp – 208-volts, 3-phase, wound rotor
   - 15 minute rated
   - nameplate current rating – 18 amperes

   A. 15.3 amperes
   B. 16.2 amperes
   C. 18.0 amperes
   D. 22.5 amperes

8. What is the power factor of a 6,500 watt load that draws 33 amperes when connected to a 240-volt, single-phase source?

    A. 1.21 percent
    B. 82 percent
    C. 68 percent
    D. 1.04 percent

9. Given: A single-phase transformer has a 240-volt primary and a 120 volt secondary. The secondary has a load of 24 amperes. The transformer is 98% efficient. What is the primary kVA rating?

    A. 5,760 kVA
    B. 2,939 kVA
    C. 294 kVA
    D. 2.94 kVA

10. A one-family dwelling with a 120/240 volt, single-phase, 200-ampere rated service has a total volt ampere rating of _____.

    A. 96,000 VA
    B. 72,000 VA
    C. 48,000 VA
    D. 24,000 VA

11. Disregarding exceptions, determine the MAXIMUM number of 120-volt fluorescent luminaires that may be installed on a 20-ampere, 120-volt lighting branch-circuit. Given: the luminaires have an amperage draw of 1.5 amperes each and are used continuously for more than 8 hours.

    A. ten
    B. eleven
    C. twelve
    D. thirteen

12. Given: A two (2) gang box will contain two (2) size 12/2 AWG with ground NM cables connected to a duplex receptacle and two (2) size 14 AWG with ground NM cables connected to a single-pole switch. The two (2) gang box will also contain four (4) cable clamps. The box is required to have a volume of at LEAST _____.

    A. 28 cubic inches
    B. 30 cubic inches
    C. 34 cubic inches
    D. 36 cubic inches

13. What is the MAXIMUM number of size 1/0 AWG THHN/THWN copper current-carrying conductors allowed in a 3 in. x 3 in. metal auxiliary gutter?

    A. nine
    B. twelve
    C. eighteen
    D. twenty-one

14. Determine the resistance, in ohms, of a 100 watt, 120-volt, incandescent light bulb.

    A. 0.833 ohms
    B. 1.20 ohms
    C. 100 ohms
    D. 144 ohms

15. Given: A residence to be constructed will have outside dimensions of 30 feet by 70 feet, including the garage. The garage measures 20 feet by 25 feet. Before taking demand factors into consideration, the house would be calculated at a MINIMUM of _____ for the general lighting and general-use receptacle load.

    A. 6,300 VA
    B. 4,800 VA
    C. 2,400 VA
    D. 2,100 VA

16. Determine the MAXIMUM number of size 500 kcmil THHW compact aluminum conductors the NEC® permits to be installed in a trade size 5 in. rigid metal conduit (RMC) nipple that is 20 inches long.

    A. ten
    B. thirteen
    C. seventeen
    D. nineteen

17. Given: A fastened in place appliance is to be served by a 20-ampere rated branch-circuit which also supplies luminaries. What is the MAXIMUM rating, in amperes, for the appliance?

    A. 10 amperes
    B. 12 amperes
    C. 16 amperes
    D. 20 amperes

18. A feeder installation consists of a 208Y/120 volt, 3-phase, 4-wire electrical system with a balanced load of fluorescent lighting. Each phase conductor has a 340 ampere load. The MINIMUM permitted ampacity of the neutral conductor for this feeder is _____.

    A. 238 amperes
    B. 275 amperes
    C. 340 amperes
    D. 680 amperes

19. Given: Eight (8) size 12 AWG THWN copper current-carrying, branch circuit conductors are to be installed in a fifty (50) foot long electrical metallic tubing (EMT) serving fluorescent lighting. Determine the ampacity of the conductors.

    A. 17.5 amperes
    B. 20.0 amperes
    C. 16.0 amperes
    D. 25.0 amperes

20. Given: A residential electric range is rated 14 kW, 240-volts, single-phase. The neutral demand load, in amperes, on the ungrounded service-entrance conductors is _____, when applying the general method of load calculations for dwelling units.

    A. 26 amperes
    B. 38 amperes
    C. 52 amperes
    D. 58 amperes

21. Determine the MINIMUM permitted trade size Schedule 80 PVC rigid conduit, more than 24 inches in length, to enclose the following conductors:

    - two – size 6 AWG with THW insulation
    - three – size 4 AWG with THWN insulation
    - three – size 1 AWG with XHHW insulation
    - one – size 6 AWG bare

    A. 1½ in.
    B. 2 in.
    C. 2½ in.
    D. 3 in.

22. A commercial building has a 208Y/120 volt, 3-phase, 4-wire electrical system. The building has eighty (80) fluorescent luminaires (lighting fixtures) with an amperage load of 1.5 amperes each, and used continuously for more than 8 hours. The building also has two (2) electric signs rated 1,500 VA each. Disregarding exceptions, determine the MINIMUM number of 120-volt, 20-ampere branch-circuits required for the lighting and sign load.

    A. seven
    B. eight
    C. nine
    D. ten

23. The MAXIMUM allowable size of a motor branch-circuit protective device that provides overcurrent protection for a size 14 AWG THWN copper motor control circuit conductor that extends from a motor controller to a start-stop push button station installed at a remote location from the controller is _____.

    A. 15 amperes
    B. 20 amperes
    C. 30 amperes
    D. 45 amperes

24. Two (2) motors with a full-load current rating of 50-amperes each are to be served by a common feeder circuit. Each motor branch-circuit will be protected by a 150 ampere non-time delay fuse. Disregarding exceptions, the feeder overcurrent protection device shall NOT be larger than _____.

    A. 150 amperes
    B. 200 amperes
    C. 250 amperes
    D. 300 amperes

25. Given: A single branch-circuit in a residence will supply two (2) 4 kVA wall-mounted ovens and one (1) 5 kVA counter-mounted cooktop in the kitchen. The cooking equipment is rated 240-volts, single-phase. Determine the MINIMUM required ampacity of the ungrounded branch circuit conductors for this home-run.

    A. 25 amperes
    B. 30 amperes
    C. 35 amperes
    D. 40 amperes

END OF EXAM 6

ELECTRICIANS PRACTICE CALCULATIONS EXAMS
EXAM 7

These questions are typical of questions encountered on Master Electricians' exams. This exam is based on the 2011 edition of the National Electrical Code®. The only material permitted for use on this type of exam is a calculator, scratch paper and a 2011 edition NEC® book. On each question select the best answer from the choices given and review your answers with the answer key included in this book.

ALLOTTED TIME: 90 minutes

1. Given: A bank building will have an 800-ampere, 480/277 volt, 3-phase, 4-wire service. The total volt ampere rating of this service is _____.

    A. 221,600 VA
    B. 383,811 VA
    C. 384,000 VA
    D. 665,088 VA

2. Disregarding exceptions, determine the MAXIMUM number of 277-volt fluorescent luminaires, with a current load of .83 amperes each, used continuously for more than eight (8) hours during the business day, that may be supplied by a 20-ampere, 277-volt lighting branch-circuit.

    A. ten
    B. thirteen
    C. nineteen
    D. twenty-four

3. Given: A two (2) gang box containing internal nonmetallic cable clamps along with a switch and receptacle is to be installed in the kitchen of a dwelling unit. The switch will connect to a size 14/2 AWG with ground NM cable from a 15-ampere circuit and the receptacle will connect to a 12/2 AWG with ground NM cable on a 20-ampere circuit. The box must have a volume of at LEAST _____.

    A. 21.5 cubic inches
    B. 22.0 cubic inches
    C. 23.5 cubic inches
    D. 25.75 cubic inches

4. One hundred (100) feet of trade size 1½ in. Schedule 40 rigid PVC conduit is to be installed above grade outdoors where there is a winter temperature of -10° F and a summer temperature of 110° F. The PVC will have an expected change in length of _____ due to expansion.

    A. 2.60 inches
    B. 4.60 inches
    C. 4.87 inches
    D. 5.07 inches

5. Given: A 3-phase transformer is rated 480/277 volts on the primary side and 208/120 volts on the secondary side. The current available on the secondary side is 225 amperes per phase. The primary current available per phase is _____.

    A. 56 amperes
    B. 98 amperes
    C. 130 amperes
    D. 390 amperes

6. A restaurant will have the following electrical kitchen equipment installed:

    - two - 20 kW ovens
    - four - 15 kW cook-tops
    - two - 5 kW dishwashers
    - one - 9 kW water heater
    - two - 5 kW booster heaters

    What is the MINIMUM demand, in kW, the NEC® permits on the ungrounded service-entrance conductors for the above listed kitchen equipment.

    A. 83.85 kW
    B. 90.30 kW
    C. 116.10 kW
    D. 129.00 kW

7. A one-family dwelling to be built will have 2,400 sq. ft. of livable space, a 800 sq. ft. unfinished basement (adaptable for future use), a 600 sq. ft. garage, a 400 sq. ft. open porch, two (2) small appliance circuits and a laundry circuit. Determine the demand load, in VA, on the ungrounded service-entrance conductors for the general lighting, and receptacle loads using the standard method of load calculation for a one-family dwelling.

    A. 6,885 VA
    B. 14,100 VA
    C. 17,100 VA
    D. 7,935 VA

8. Disregarding exceptions, the ampacity of the phase conductors from the terminals of a 15 kVA, 240-volt, single-phase generator to the first overcurrent device protecting the load shall be at LEAST _____.

    A. 63 amperes
    B. 72 amperes
    C. 78 amperes
    D. 94 amperes

9. A 60 hp, 3-phase, 480-volt, synchronous type motor has a 90 percent power factor. According to the NEC®, what is its full-load running current?

    A. 78.00 amperes
    B. 76.25 amperes
    C. 61.00 amperes
    D. 67.10 amperes

10. Given: A 150 kVA, transformer with a 208Y/120 volt, 3-phase, 4-wire secondary has 2 percent impedance. Determine the MAXIMUM fault current available at the secondary terminals of the transformer.

    A. 10,400 amperes
    B. 18,334 amperes
    C. 20,800 amperes
    D. 36,057 amperes

Copyright 2016

BrownTechnical.org

11. Where a single-phase, 30-ampere, 240-volt branch-circuit has a load of 24 amperes and is located 150 feet from the panelboard, determine the MINIMUM size THWN copper conductors required to limit the voltage drop to 7 volts.

    A. 10 AWG
    B. 8 AWG
    C. 6 AWG
    D. 4 AWG

12. A department store has 120 feet of show window lighting operating on 120-volt circuits of a 208Y/120 volt, 3-phase system. Disregarding exceptions, calculate the MINIMUM number of 120-volt, 20-ampere lighting branch-circuits required for the show window lighting.

    A. twenty
    B. sixteen
    C. thirteen
    D. ten

13. A 3-phase, 240-volt, 7½ hp, Design B, 50°C rise motor has a full-load ampere rating of 20 amperes marked on the nameplate. The overload devices used to protect this motor shall be selected to trip at a MAXIMUM value of not more than _____.

    A. 26.0 amperes
    B. 23.0 amperes
    C. 28.6 amperes
    D. 25.3 amperes

14. The cost of operating a 200 watt lamp for 8 hours at 9 cents per kWH is _____.

    A. $1.44
    B. $1.84
    C. $0.44
    D. $0.14

15. A permitted by the NEC®, what is the MINIMUM standard amperage rating of a circuit breaker used as the motor disconnecting means for a 40 hp, 208-volt, 3-phase, continuous-duty, squirrel cage motor?

    A. 125 amperes
    B. 150 amperes
    C. 175 amperes
    D. 200 amperes

16. Given: Only the shell of an office building is to be built. The building is 225 feet long and 90 feet wide and 10 stories high. The number of receptacles to be installed is not yet determined. Calculate the general lighting and general-use receptacle demand, in VA, on the ungrounded service-entrance conductors. The service overcurrent device and its assembly are listed for operation at 100 percent of their rating. The service is 480Y/277 volt, 3-phase.

    A. 911,250 VA
    B. 810,000 VA
    C. 708,750 VA
    D. 607,500 VA

17. Refer to the above question. Determine the MINIMUM number of 20 ampere, 277-volt, general lighting branch-circuits required. Consider that branch circuit breakers of this size are not rated for continuous use.

    A. 295 lighting circuits
    B. 128 lighting circuits
    C. 175 lighting circuits
    D. 160 lighting circuits

18. Determine the MINIMUM size THHN copper branch-circuit conductors required to supply a continuous-duty, 40 hp, 460-volt, 3-phase, Design C motor. The motor is on the end of a short conduit run that only contains three (3) conductors operating at an expected ambient temperature of 50° C. Consider all terminations to be rated 75° C.

    A. 6 AWG
    B. 4 AWG
    C. 2 AWG
    D. 3 AWG

19. Determine the ampacity of size 1/0 AWG THHW copper conductors when used as service-entrance conductors, installed in a conduit mast, on a retail building given the following:

    - wet location
    - 4 current-carrying conductors in the conduit
    - conduit length 6 feet
    - ambient temperature 110° F

    A. 98 amperes
    B. 112 amperes
    C. 123 amperes
    D. 150 amperes

20. Determine the MINIMUM size ladder type cable tray width required for the following combination of listed single conductors rated 600 volts:

    - twenty – size 500 kcmil with THWN insulation
    - thirty – size 250 kcmil with THWN insulation

    A. 24 inches
    B. 30 inches
    C. 36 inches
    D. 42 inches

21. Given: A trade size 3½ in. rigid metal conduit (RMC) contains four (4) size 350 kcmil THWN copper conductors. This conduit is filled to _____.

    A. 21 percent
    B. 30 percent
    C. 40 percent
    D. 53 percent

22. Given: There will be three (3) conductors in a conduit to supply the motor of an overhead bridge crane. The crane has one 25 hp, 460-volt, 3-phase motor only, with a 15 minute rating. Determine the MINIMUM size copper, THWN conductors permitted by the NEC® to supply this motor.

    A. 12 AWG
    B. 10 AWG
    C. 8 AWG
    D. 6 AWG

23. The absolute MAXIMUM rating of an inverse time circuit breaker for branch-circuit, short-circuit and ground-fault protection allowed for a 40 hp, 230-volt, 3-phase continuous-duty, Design B motor is _____.

    A. 350 amperes
    B. 250 amperes
    C. 300 amperes
    D. 400 amperes

24. Determine the MINIMUM size THWN copper conductors required for a feeder supplying ten (10) 240 volt, single-phase, 12 kVA electric ranges in a restaurant kitchen of a casino/hotel.

    A. 2 AWG
    B. 1 AWG
    C. 350 kcmil
    D. 400 kcmil

25. A 10 kVA single-phase, 240-volt, central heating unit is connected to a single-phase 208-volt system. Determine the approximate VA rating of the unit when connected to the lower voltage.

    A. 5,800 VA
    B. 7,500 VA
    C. 7,200 VA
    D. 6,900 VA

END OF EXAM 7

ELECTRICIANS PRACTICE CALCULATIONS EXAMS
EXAM 8

These questions are typical of questions encountered on Master Electricians' exams. This exam is based on the 2011 edition of the National Electrical Code®. The only material permitted for use on this type of exam is a calculator, scratch paper and a 2011 edition NEC® book. On each question select the best answer from the choices given and review your answers with the answer key included in this book.

ALLOTTED TIME: 90 minutes

1. What is the MINIMUM trade size electrical metallic tubing (EMT) required for the following listed copper conductors installed in a 26 inch long conduit?

   - six – size 3 AWG THWN
   - three – size 8 AWG THW
   - two – size 10 AWG THW

   A. 1¼ in.
   B. 1½ in.
   C. 2 in.
   D. 2½ in.

2. Given: You are to build a 208Y/120 volt, 3-phase, 4-wire, 200 ampere rated service on the exterior of a commercial building. The conductors are to be installed in an eight (8) foot long conduit mast where the ambient temperature is 110° F. Assume all conductors to be current-carrying. Determine the MINIMUM size 75ºC rated copper conductors the NEC® requires for this service.

   A. 250 kcmil
   B. 300 kcmil
   C. 350 kcmil
   D. 400 kcmil

3. Determine the MAXIMUM standard size time-delay fuse rating the NEC® permits for overcurrent protection of a 208-volt, 3-phase, 60 ampere, hermetic refrigerant motor-compressor.

   A. 100 amperes
   B. 125 amperes
   C. 135 amperes
   D. 150 amperes

4. A multifamily dwelling unit consists of thirty (30) dwelling units with a 120/240 volt, 6 kW clothes dryer in each unit. What is the dryer load feeder demand of the line and neutral for the apartment complex?

   A. Line 180,000 VA – Neutral 54,000 VA
   B. Line 91,800 VA – Neutral 54,000 VA
   C. Line 54,000 VA – Neutral 37,800 VA
   D. Line 56,700 VA – Neutral 39,690 VA

5. The branch-circuit demand load, in kW, for a 21.6 kW electric range installed in a residence is _____.

   A. 17.6 kW
   B. 12 kW
   C. 10.4 kW
   D. 8 kW

6. Given: A 240-volt, single-phase motor draws 28 amperes and has a 55 percent efficiency rating. The horsepower rating of the motor is _____.

   A. 7½ hp
   B. 5 hp
   C. 3 hp
   D. 2 hp

7. A one-family dwelling has the following appliances fastened in place:

    - one – sump pump rated @ 240-volts, 5 amperes
    - one – dishwasher rated @ 1,200 VA
    - one – garbage disposer rated @ 900 VA
    - one - garage door opener rated @ 800 VA

    The demand, in VA, on the ungrounded service-entrance conductors for the listed appliances is _____, when using the standard method of load calculation for one-family dwellings.

    A. 4,100 VA
    B. 4,400 VA
    C. 3,075 VA
    D. 3,300 VA

8. The branch-circuit conductors supplying a 240-volt, single-phase, 15 kW rated fixed electric space heater provided with a 10 ampere blower motor are required to have an ampacity of at LEAST _____ .

    A. 63 amperes
    B. 78 amperes
    C. 91 amperes
    D. 109 amperes

9. Given: You are to install twelve (12) size 8 AWG THWN copper conductors in a trade size 1¼ in. rigid metal conduit (RMC). Determine the ampacity of the conductors given the following related information:

    - ambient temperature is 105° F
    - conduit length is 80 feet
    - nine (9) conductors are current-carrying

    A. 20.5 amperes
    B. 28.7 amperes
    C. 30.8 amperes
    D. 32.8 amperes

10. Three (3) four-conductor cables with size 2/0 AWG THHN copper conductors are installed in a solid bottom cable tray with a continuous cover. The conductors are all current-carrying and they do not exceed the permitted cable tray fill. The conductors are rated for 600 volts. What is the ampacity of the individual conductors?

    A. 195.00 amperes
    B. 185.25 amperes
    C. 156.00 amperes
    D. 148.20 amperes

11. The MINIMUM permitted amperage rating of the conductors that supply a 240-volt, 3-phase, generator-type arc welder that has a 140 ampere primary with an 80 percent duty-cycle is _____.

    A. 175 amperes
    B. 140 amperes
    C. 127 amperes
    D. 112 amperes

12. Which of the following square metal junction boxes would be the MINIMUM permitted for the installation of six (6) size 10 AWG conductors and three (3) size 6 AWG conductors? Given: All the conductors are current-carrying and the box contains no devices or internal clamps and has a flat blank cover.

    A. 4" x 1¼"
    B. 4" x 1½"
    C. 4" x 2⅛"
    D. 4¾" x 1½"

13. In regard to a 208-volt, 3-phase, 10 hp, Design C, squirrel cage, continuous-duty motor, determine the absolute MAXIMUM standard rating of an adjustable instantaneous trip circuit breaker the NEC® permits for branch-circuit, short-circuit and ground-fault protection for the motor. The circuit breaker is part of a listed combination motor controller having overload protection in each conductor.

    A. 75 amperes
    B. 80 amperes
    C. 250 amperes
    D. 400 amperes

14. Determine the MINIMUM number of 20-ampere, 277-volt, general lighting branch-circuits required for a 150,000 sq. ft. department store where the actual connected lighting load is 400 kVA. No exceptions are applicable.

    A. 72
    B. 82
    C. 91
    D. 102

15. When building the service for a mobile home park that has electrical provisions for a total of 48 mobile home sites, the plans require the MINIMUM VA rating of the individual sites to be as follows:

    - 34 sites @ 24,000 VA each
    - 8 sites @ 14,400 VA each
    - 6 sites @ 12,000 VA each

    The ungrounded service-entrance conductors for the main service of the mobile home park shall have a current-carrying capacity of at LEAST _____.

    A. 4,334 amperes
    B. 746 amperes
    C. 961 amperes
    D. 997 amperes

16. What is the MAXIMUM overcurrent device rating, in amperes, permitted to protect a nonmotor appliance with a FLA rating of 60 amperes?

    A. 48 amperes
    B. 60 amperes
    C. 75 amperes
    D. 90 amperes

17. How many size 12 AWG conductors may be installed in a 3½ inch deep, 4-gang masonry box that contains two (2) three-way switches and two (2) single-pole switches?

    A. 28
    B. 26
    C. 36
    D. 32

18. A three-phase, 208-volt, 15 hp, induction type, continuous-duty motor is located 230 feet from the motor control center. The branch-circuit conductors serving the motor are copper, size 6 AWG with THWN-2 insulation. Determine the approximate voltage drop on the branch circuit conductors. (K = 12.9)

    A. 9 volts
    B. 12 volts
    C. 15 volts
    D. 18 volts

19. A 120/240 volt, single-phase, 3-wire feeder serves a panelboard supplying 120-volt and 240-volt single-phase non-continuous equipment. The ungrounded conductors have a calculated load of 150 amperes and the neutral conductor has a calculated load of 110 amperes. The feeder will consist of copper conductors installed in a dry location. Which one of the following combination of conductors is permitted by the NEC®? Consider all terminations to be rated 75°C.

    A. Two size 1 AWG THHN with a size 2 AWG THW neutral
    B. Two size 1 AWG THHN with a size 1 AWG THHN neutral
    C. Two size 1/0 AWG THW with a size 3 AWG THHN neutral
    D. Two size 1/0 AWG THW with a size 2 AWG THW neutral

20. What MINIMUM size THW copper conductors are required for a 25 foot tap from 500 kcmil THW copper feeder conductors protected by a 400 ampere inverse time circuit breaker without installing overcurrent protection at the point of the tap?

    A. 2 AWG
    B. 1 AWG
    C. 1/0 AWG
    D. 2/0 AWG

21. In a high school welding shop, a 120/240 volt, single-phase, feeder circuit is to supply four (4) transformer arc welders each with a 50% duty-cycle. The welders have primary current ratings of 60 amperes, 50 amperes, 40 amperes and 30 amperes. The feeder conductors supplying the welders must have a MINIMUM current-carrying capacity of _____.

    A. 180 amperes
    B. 128 amperes
    C. 118 amperes
    D. 102 amperes

22. Determine the MINIMUM size THWN copper feeder conductors required by the NEC® to supply the following 480-volt, continuous-duty, 3-phase, induction type, Design C, ac motors. Assume terminations to be rated 75°C.

    - two – 50 hp
    - one – 40 hp

    A. 2/0 AWG
    B. 3/0 AWG
    C. 4/0 AWG
    D. 250 kcmil

23. A recreational vehicle park with a 120/240 volt, single-phase electrical system will have a total of forty (40) sites, all with electrical power. Using the MINIMUM requirements mandated by the NEC® for RV parks, determine the MINIMUM size service required when using standard ampere ratings of fuses for overcurrent protection.

    A. 600 amperes
    B. 250 amperes
    C. 350 amperes
    D. 400 amperes

24. A 240-volt, single-phase, 21.85 kW commercial cooking appliance is to be supplied by copper branch-circuit conductors with a 60°C temperature rating. Which of the following is the MINIMUM allowable size of the conductors?

    A. 3 AWG
    B. 2 AWG
    C. 1 AWG
    D. 1/0 AWG

25. The allowable ampacity of a size 750 kcmil XHHW aluminum conductor when there are six (6) current-carrying conductors in the raceway, installed in a dry location, with an ambient temperature of 22°C, is _____.

    A. 323.40 amperes
    B. 365.40 amperes
    C. 361.92 amperes
    D. 348.00 amperes

END OF EXAM 8

ELECTRICIANS PRACTICE CALCULATIONS EXAMS EXAM 9

These questions are typical of questions encountered on Master Electricians' exams. This exam is based on the 2011 edition of the National Electrical Code®. The only material permitted for use on this type of exam is a calculator, scratch paper and a 2011 edition NEC® book. On each question select the best answer from the choices given and review your answers with the answer key included in this book.

ALLOTTED TIME: 90 minutes

1. Determine the resistance per foot, in ohms, of a conductor given the following information:

   - total length of conductor is 300 feet
   - total voltage drop is 6.3 volts
   - circuit load is 15 amperes

   A. 0.0014 ohms
   B. 0.4133 ohms
   C. 1,890 ohms
   D. 4,500 ohms

2. What is the connected general lighting and receptacle load, in VA, of an office building with an area of 4,500 square feet and the actual number of general-use receptacle outlets to be installed is not yet determined?

   A. 13,500 VA
   B. 15,750 VA
   C. 18,000 VA
   D. 20,250 VA

3. Refer to the above question. Disregarding exceptions, determine the MINIMUM number of 120-volt, 20-ampere branch-circuits the NEC® requires for the lighting and the general-use receptacles.

   A. eleven
   B. ten
   C. nine
   D. eight

4. Determine the MAXIMUM number of size 500 kcmil THW copper current-carrying conductors that may be installed in an 8 inch x 8 inch metal wireway.

    A. fourteen
    B. fifteen
    C. sixteen
    D. seventeen

5. What is the neutral demand load, in amperes, for a one-family dwelling with a total connected line load of 65 kVA and a neutral load of 50 kVA? The service is 120/240 volts, single-phase.

    A. 270.8 amperes
    B. 208.3 amperes
    C. 205.8 amperes
    D. 189.6 amperes

6. Given: A 480-volt, 3-phase feeder is to supply a 150 kVA fixed electric space heating load. Disregarding exceptions, what is the MINIMUM ampacity of the conductors supplying the space heating load the NEC® requires?

    A. 180 amperes
    B. 226 amperes
    C. 313 amperes
    D. 391 amperes

7. Given: A 120-volt, single-phase, branch-circuit has a load of 10 amperes. The total circuit conductor length is 500 feet. The wire has a resistance of 1.75 ohms per 1,000 feet. What is the approximate voltage drop in the conductors of this circuit?

    A. 9 volts
    B. 12 volts
    C. 18 volts
    D. 120 volts

8. What is the calculated feeder demand load for a dwelling unit that has the following cooking equipment:

   - 8 kVA oven
   - 6 kVA oven
   - 3.5 kVA oven
   - 6 kVA cooktop unit
   - 3.5 kVA counter-mounted broiler

   A. 12.2 kVA
   B. 18.6 kVA
   C. 27.3 kVA
   D. 29.7 kVA

9. Determine the approximate horsepower of a 3-phase, 208-volt, Design B, ac electric motor that draws 22 amperes of current, has an 87 percent power factor and an efficiency of 81 percent.

   A. 3 hp
   B. 5 hp
   C. 7½ hp
   D. 10 hp

10. You are to install ninety (90) feet of multioutlet assembly in the appliance sales area of a department store where the appliances are likely to be used simultaneously. Determine the MINIMUM number of 20 ampere, 120-volt, single-phase, branch-circuits required to supply this multioutlet assembly.

    A. four
    B. five
    C. six
    D. seven

11. A three-phase, 480-volt, 100 ampere non-continuous load is located 390 feet from a panelboard. What MINIMUM size THWN aluminum conductors are required to limit the voltage drop to 3 percent?
    (K = 21.2)

    A. 2 AWG
    B. 1 AWG
    C. 1/0 AWG
    D. 2/0 AWG

12. Determine the MINIMUM size THWN copper feeder conductors required by the NEC® to supply the following 480-volt, continuous-duty, 3-phase, induction type, Design C, motors.

    - 1 – 40 hp
    - 1 – 50 hp
    - 1 – 60 hp

    A. 2/0 AWG
    B. 3/0 AWG
    C. 4/0 AWG
    D. 250 kcmil

13. What is the ampacity of a size 10 THW copper current-carrying conductor, when four (4) of them are pulled into a 25 ft. long conduit and the ambient temperature is 50°C? Consider all conductors contained within the raceway are current-carrying.

    A. 21 amperes
    B. 26 amperes
    C. 28 amperes
    D. 30 amperes

14. The absolute MAXIMUM rating of an inverse time breaker for branch-circuit, short-circuit and ground-fault protection allowed for a 50 hp, 3-phase, 480-volt, continuous-duty motor is _____.

    A. 200 amperes
    B. 225 amperes
    C. 250 amperes
    D. 260 amperes

15. Determine the MAXIMUM number of size 14 AWG THHN copper conductors permitted by the NEC® that may be installed in a trade size 1 inch rigid metal conduit (RMC) nipple that is 12 inches long.

    A. thirty
    B. thirty-six
    C. fifty-four
    D. fifty-five

16. Determine the MINIMUM required length of a junction box that has a 3½ inch conduit containing size 250 kcmil conductors, pulled through the box for a 90° angle pull. Disregard exceptions.

    A. 21 inches
    B. 24 inches
    C. 28 inches
    D. 34 inches

17. What is the MINIMUM size THWN copper conductors required to supply a continuous-duty, 25 hp, 208-volt, 3-phase motor? Given: The expected ambient temperature is 50°C and consider all terminations to be rated for 75°C.

    A. 6 AWG
    B. 3 AWG
    C. 2 AWG
    D. 1 AWG

18. An existing office building with a 208Y/120 volt, 3-phase, 4-wire service has 250 general-purpose duplex receptacles added. What MINIMUM demand, in amperes, would be added to the ungrounded service-entrance conductors for the receptacles?

    A. 125 amperes
    B. 100 amperes
    C. 76 amperes
    D. 69 amperes

19. A 480Y/277 volt, 3-phase, 4-wire service has three (3) size 500 kcmil THWN aluminum conductors paralleled per phase. What MINIMUM size copper grounding electrode conductor does the NEC® mandate from the service equipment to the building steel used as the grounding electrode?

    A. 1/0 AWG
    B. 2/0 AWG
    C. 3/0 AWG
    D. 4/0 AWG

20. Where a rooftop mounted air-conditioning unit is supplied with three (3) size 8 AWG THWN copper conductors, enclosed in an electrical metallic tubing (EMT) within three (3) inches of the rooftop, and exposed to direct sunlight and an ambient temperature of 100 degrees F, the allowable ampacity of the conductors is _____ .

    A. 50 amperes
    B. 44 amperes
    C. 29 amperes
    D. 25 amperes

21. A feeder circuit is to supply the following 480-volt, 3-phase, intermittent use cooking related equipment in a restaurant:

    - 1 – 5,000 VA booster heater
    - 1 – 5,000 VA grill
    - 4 – 3,000 VA fryers
    - 2 – 6,000 VA ovens

    Each ungrounded conductor in this feeder circuit must have a MINIMUM ampacity of _____.

    A. 41 amperes
    B. 18 amperes
    C. 21 amperes
    D. 27 amperes

22. Determine the MINIMUM size junction box required, in cubic inches, for the following combination of conductors, when the box has a flat blank cover and contains no devices or clamps:

    - 3 – size 10 AWG ungrounded conductors
    - 1 – size 10 AWG grounded conductor
    - 1 – size 10 AWG grounding conductor
    - 3 – size 12 AWG ungrounded conductors
    - 1 – size 12 AWG grounded conductor
    - 1 – size 12 AWG grounding conductor

    A. 21.50 cubic inches
    B. 23.75 cubic inches
    C. 25.00 cubic inches
    D. 19.25 cubic inches

23. When applying the optional method of load calculation, after taking demand factors into consideration, the demand load, in kVA, for a 20,000 square foot school building with a total connected load of 680 kVA is _____.

    A. 170 kVA
    B. 385 kVA
    C. 575 kVA
    D. 680 kVA

24. Determine the conductor ampacity given the following conditions:

    - conductors are size 10 AWG THWN copper.
    - two sets of 3-phase, 4-wire, 208Y/120 volt, branch-circuits are contained in the same conduit.
    - the load being served is information technology equipment.
    - ambient temperature is 86°F.

    A. 20.0 amperes
    B. 24.5 amperes
    C. 30.0 amperes
    D. 35.0 amperes

25. Determine the approximate additional load, per phase, that may be added to a transformer where given the following information:

    - transformer is rated 150 kVA.
    - transformer existing load is 200 amperes per phase.
    - voltage is 208Y/120, 3-phase, 4-wire.

    A. 196 amperes
    B. 216 amperes
    C. 240 amperes
    D. 416 amperes

END OF EXAM 9

ELECTRICIANS PRACTICE CALCULATIONS EXAMS
EXAM 10

These questions are typical of questions encountered on Master Electricians' exams. This exam is based on the 2011 edition of the National Electrical Code®. The only material permitted for use on this type of exam is a calculator, scratch paper and a 2011 edition NEC® book. On each question select the best answer from the choices given and review your answers with the answer key included in this book.

ALLOTTED TIME: 90 minutes

1. Where a 240-volt, 3-phase branch-circuit has an 80 percent power factor and the intensity of the current is 25 amperes, how much power is transmitted through the circuit?

    A. 7,200 VA
    B. 7,960 VA
    C. 8,314 VA
    D. 4,800 VA

2. Given: An existing ninety (90) foot long, trade size 1 inch, Schedule 40 rigid PVC conduit contains two (2) size 8 AWG THWN conductors and one (1) size 10 AWG THWN conductor. How many additional size 10 AWG THWN conductors are permitted to be installed in the PVC?

    A. eight
    B. nine
    C. ten
    D. eleven

3. What is the demand load, in kW, on the ungrounded service-entrance conductors of an apartment complex that has thirty five (35), 10 kW ranges installed in the dwelling units? (Use the general method of load calculation for dwelling units.)

    A. 280 kW
    B. 67.2 kW
    C. 61.5 kW
    D. 50.0 kW

4. In general, how many 20-ampere, 277-volt, general-lighting branch circuits are required by the NEC® for a 150,000 square feet department store?

    A. 42
    B. 82
    C. 102
    D. 150

5. Given: A 240-volt, single-phase, feeder has a 100 ampere continuous load protected with a 125-ampere rated circuit breaker. The load is 150 feet from the switchboard. Where size 1 AWG THWN/THHN copper conductors are used as the feeder conductors, what is the approximate voltage drop on this circuit? (K = 12.9)

    A. 2 volts
    B. 4 volts
    C. 7 volts
    D. 12 volts

6. In general, the disconnecting means for a 50 hp, 480-volt, 3-phase, continuous-duty, induction-type ac motor shall have an ampere rating of at LEAST _____.

    A. 63 amperes
    B. 75 amperes
    C. 91 amperes
    D. 126 amperes

7. A commercial occupancy is to have a fifteen (15) ton A/C unit with a full load current rating of 100 amperes and a thirty (30) kW electric heating unit installed; both units are 208-volts, 3-phase. What is the MINIMUM demand load, in amperes, to be applied on the service for the A/C and heating equipment?

    A. 100 amperes
    B. 125 amperes
    C. 150 amperes
    D. 83 amperes

8. Where there are three (3), 3-wire, 120/240 volt multi-wire branch circuits in a conduit serving multioutlet cord-and-plug connected loads and the conductors are size 10 AWG THW copper, what is the MAXIMUM standard rating of the overcurrent protection as permitted by the NEC® for these branch-circuits?

    A. 20 amperes
    B. 25 amperes
    C. 30 amperes
    D. 35 amperes

9. Given: Six (6) size 6 AWG THW copper conductors are installed in the same raceway with six (6) size 6 AWG XHHW copper conductors. The MAXIMUM permitted ampacity for the size 6 AWG XHHW conductors is _____, where all the conductors are current-carrying.

    A. 25.0 amperes
    B. 32.5 amperes
    C. 38.5 amperes
    D. 45.5 amperes

10. Determine the MINIMUM size THW ungrounded conductors required to supply a 25 hp, continuous-duty, squirrel cage, 3-phase motor rated @ 50°C temperature rise, operating on a 240-volt system. Consider all terminations are rated for 75°C.

    A. 6 AWG
    B. 4 AWG
    C. 3 AWG
    D. 2 AWG

11. For a transformer vault ventilated by natural circulation of air to an outdoor area, what MINIMUM size vent is required for a transformer vault that houses a 50 kVA transformer?

    A. 1 square foot
    B. 50 square inches
    C. 150 square inches
    D. 330 square inches

12. A 60 unit apartment complex has a 120/240 volt, single-phase service where each unit has a 120-volt, 1,200 VA dishwasher installed. What is the service demand load for the dishwashers, in amperes, on the ungrounded service-entrance conductors? Use the standard method of load calculation.

    A. 225 amperes
    B. 300 amperes
    C. 450 amperes
    D. 600 amperes

13. Given: A 15 kVA, three-phase, transformer has a 480-volt primary and a 208Y/120 volt secondary. When primary protection only is needed, what is the MAXIMUM standard rating for the primary protection circuit breaker?

    A. 20 amperes
    B. 25 amperes
    C. 35 amperes
    D. 60 amperes

14. A circuit breaker provided to protect an air-conditioning condensing unit with a rated current of 35 amperes indicated on the nameplate, is required to have a MAXIMUM ampere rating of no more than _____.

    A. 60 amperes
    B. 80 amperes
    C. 75 amperes
    D. 70 amperes

15. What MINIMUM voltage is required to be available for up to 1½ hours, when using storage batteries serving emergency lighting, if the normal voltage is 120-volts?

    A. 60 volts
    B. 90 volts
    C. 105 volts
    D. 120 volts

16. Where a panelboard contains thirty (30), 20-ampere, single-pole circuit breakers only, the MAXIMUM standard size overcurrent protection permitted to protect this panelboard is _____.

    A. 200 amperes
    B. 225 amperes
    C. 400 amperes
    D. 600 amperes

17. Determine the MAXIMUM number of size 4 AWG THHN conductors permitted to be installed in a trade size 1½ in. intermediate metal conduit (IMC) nipple, 18 inches long.

    A. twelve
    B. fourteen
    C. fifteen
    D. sixteen

18. Given: A trade size 2 inch electrical metallic tubing (EMT) contains four (4) size 1/0 AWG THWN conductors only; determine the percentage of fill for this installation.

    A. 14 percent
    B. 22 percent
    C. 40 percent
    D. 53 percent

19. What is the approximate MAXIMUM distance a single-phase, 240-volt, 42 ampere load may be located from a panelboard to limit the voltage-drop to 7 volts, when given the following related information?

    - copper conductors
    - K = 12.9
    - size 8 AWG THWN conductors

    A. 50 feet
    B. 110 feet
    C. 160 feet
    D. 195 feet

20. Determine the MAXIMUM number of size 350 kcmil THW copper single conductors permitted to be installed in a 12 inch wide ladder type cable tray.

    A. twenty-one (21)
    B. twenty-two (22)
    C. twenty-three (23)
    D. twenty-four (24)

21. When used as a disconnecting means, what is the MINIMUM standard size circuit breaker that may be installed for a 10 hp, 230-volt, 3-phase air conditioning unit?

    A. 25 amperes
    B. 30 amperes
    C. 35 amperes
    D. 40 amperes

22. What is the MINIMUM demand load of the clothes dryers, in VA, for the grounded (neutral) service-entrance conductor of a 12 unit multifamily dwelling having a 5.5 kW clothes dryer in each unit? Use the general method of load calculation for dwelling units.

    A. 19,700 VA
    B. 21,252 VA
    C. 30,360 VA
    D. 46,200 VA

23. Determine the MINIMUM size copper grounded conductor required for a 208Y/120 volt, 3-phase, 4-wire service with three (3) paralleled size 600 AWG THWN copper ungrounded conductors per phase, installed in three (3) conduits.

    A. 1/0 AWG
    B. 2/0 AWG
    C. 3/0 AWG
    D. 4/0 AWG

24. When applying the optional method of load calculations for new restaurants, determine the MAXIMUM standard size main circuit breaker required for a restaurant that is all electric, with a total connected load of 330 kVA, and a 208Y/120 volt, 3-phase, 4-wire service.

    A. 700 amperes
    B. 600 amperes
    C. 500 amperes
    D. 450 amperes

25. What is the MINIMUM size THW copper conductors required to supply a 7½ hp, single-phase, continuous-duty, 240-volt motor that is 200 feet from the panelboard? Limit voltage drop to 3 percent and consider all terminations to be rated 75°C. (K = 12.9)

    A. 6 AWG
    B. 4 AWG
    C. 8 AWG
    D. 2 AWG

END OF EXAM 10

ELECTRICIANS PRACTICE CALCULATIONS EXAMS
FINAL EXAM

These questions are typical of questions encountered on all Electricians' exams. This exam is based on the 2011 edition of the National Electrical Code®. The only material permitted for use on this type of exam is a calculator, scratch paper and a 2011 edition NEC® book. On each question select the best answer from the choices given and review your answers with the answer key included in this book. Passing grade for Journeyman Electricians on this test is 70%; passing grade for Master Electricians is 75%. Questions are valued at one point each.

ALLOTTED TIME: 6 hours

1. What is the required volume, in cubic inches, for a junction box that contains the following combination of conductors?

    - 2 – size 10 AWG ungrounded conductors
    - 1 – size 10 AWG grounded conductor
    - 1 – size 10 AWG grounding conductor
    - 2 – size 12 AWG ungrounded conductors
    - 1 – size 12 AWG grounded conductor
    - 1 – size 12 AWG grounding conductor

    A. 14.50 cubic inches
    B. 16.75 cubic inches
    C. 17.50 cubic inches
    D. 19.00 cubic inches

2. Determine the MINIMUM number of 120-volt, 20-ampere branch-circuits required for general lighting and general-purpose receptacles for a 20,000 sq. ft. apartment building that is not designed for permanent residents and cooking facilities for tenants are not available.

    A. twenty-five
    B. thirty-two
    C. sixteen
    D. seventeen

3. Determine the MINIMUM size USE aluminum cable permitted for use on an underground installed 120/240 volt, single-phase, service for a small office building that has a total load of 23,600 VA after all demand factors have been taken into consideration. Consider all terminations are rated 75°C.

    A. 1/0 AWG
    B. 2/0 AWG
    C. 1 AWG
    D. 2 AWG

4. Given: A feeder will supply a continuous lighting load of 39 amperes and a motor load of 24 amperes. The feeder must have an ampacity of at LEAST_____.

    A. 63 amperes
    B. 69 amperes
    C. 73 amperes
    D. 79 amperes

5. When calculating the total load for a residence, before taking demand factors into consideration, what MINIMUM VA must be included where the home has two (2) bathrooms, one (1) laundry and three (3) small appliance circuits?

    A. 9,000 VA
    B. 4,500 VA
    C. 6,000 VA
    D. 7,500 VA

6. Given: A retail department store has forty-six (46) linear feet of show window display lighting at the front of the store. How many receptacle outlets does the NEC® require for the show window lighting?

    A. six
    B. four
    C. two
    D. one

7. The MAXIMUM allowable ampacity of a size 10 AWG THHW copper current-carrying conductor when there are not more than three (3) conductors installed in a conduit in a dry location, and the surrounding temperature is 90° F, is _____.

    A. 36.40 amperes
    B. 33.60 amperes
    C. 31.85 amperes
    D. 38.40 amperes

8. What is the approximate horsepower rating of a 240-volt, single-phase motor that draws 18.5 amperes of current, with an efficiency of 85%?

    A. 3½ hp
    B. 5 hp
    C. 10 hp
    D. 7½ hp

9. Where installing a service lateral for a one-family dwelling in a housing development, the residence is to be supplied with the following service-entrance conductors:

    - two - 3/0 AWG XHHW compact aluminum ungrounded conductors
    - one - 1/0 AWG THHW compact aluminum grounded conductor
    - one – 6 AWG bare stranded copper conductor

    Determine the MINIMUM trade size Schedule 40 rigid PVC conduit the NEC® requires to enclose the service-entrance conductors.

    A. 3 in.
    B. 2½ in.
    C. 2 in.
    D. 1½ in.

10. Given: A conduit is to contain six (6) size 2/0 AWG THWN copper ungrounded conductors and two (2) size 2/0 AWG THWN copper grounded conductors (neutrals) that have harmonic currents present. The terminations are rated 75°C and the ambient temperature is 86°F. Determine the allowable ampacity of these current-carrying conductors.

    A. 112.5 amperes
    B. 122.5 amperes
    C. 142.2 amperes
    D. 162.5 amperes

11. Determine the total resistance of a conductor given the following related information:

    - Source voltage at the panelboard is 120 volts.
    - Voltage at the load is 114 volts.
    - Circuit load is 16 amperes.
    - Conductor length is 125 feet.

    A. 3.00 ohms
    B. 0.375 ohms
    C. 0.166 ohms
    D. 0.002 ohms

12. Determine the MINIMUM ampacity the NEC® requires of the branch circuit conductors serving a continuous-duty, 208-volt, 3-phase, 15 hp induction type motor.

    A. 38.50 amperes
    B. 53.13 amperes
    C. 57.75 amperes
    D. 60.06 amperes

13. Given: A group of ten (10) conductors having a cross-sectional area of 0.836 square inches are to be installed in a Schedule 40 rigid PVC conduit that is in excess of 24 inches in length. The NEC® mandates a MINIMUM standard trade size of _____ PVC to be used for this installation.

    A. 1¼ in.
    B. 1½ in.
    C. 2 in.
    D. 2½ in.

14. Determine the full-load amperes (FLA) of a 2,000 watt, 3-phase, 208 volt motor that has an 80 percent power factor.

    A. 6.94 amperes
    B. 4.44 amperes
    C. 12.04 amperes
    D. 7.69 amperes

15. The MAXIMUM allowable ampacity of a current-carrying size 12 AWG THWN copper conductor is _____, when the ambient temperature is 42°C and six (6) additional current-carrying conductors of the same size and insulation are in the conduit.

    A. 16.40 amperes
    B. 14.35 amperes
    C. 11.48 amperes
    D. 13.12 amperes

16. A one-family dwelling has 2½ bathrooms, 1 laundry and a kitchen. Determine the MINIMUM number of 20-ampere, 120-volt, branch-circuits the NEC® requires for the receptacle outlets in the listed rooms.

    A. three
    B. four
    C. five
    D. six

17. A 3-phase, 208-volt, 7,500 VA commercial rated electric fryer located in a restaurant will have a full-load current rating of _____ .

    A. 16.4 amperes
    B. 20.8 amperes
    C. 36.0 amperes
    D. 62.5 amperes

18. A 4.5 kW, 240-volt, clothes dryer in a residence will add an additional _____ to the demand on the ungrounded (line) service-entrance conductors on a 120/240 volt, single-phase service.

    A. 20.80 amperes
    B. 18.75 amperes
    C. 41.61 amperes
    D. 37.50 amperes

19. A commercial kitchen will have the following cooking related equipment installed:

    - one – 30 kW range
    - one – 20 kW water heater
    - one – 5 kW booster heater

    What is the demand factor, in kW, that should be applied to the ungrounded service-entrance conductors for the cooking equipment?

    A. 50.0 kW
    B. 44.0 kW
    C. 49.5 kW
    D. 55.0 kW

20. What is the full-load current rating on the secondary side of a 75 kVA, 3-phase transformer having a 480/277 volt, primary and a 208Y/120 volt secondary?

    A. 90 amperes
    B. 208 amperes
    C. 277 amperes
    D. 361 amperes

21. A kitchen with a demand load of 54,000 VA is to be added to an existing church. The church is provided with a 3-phase, 208Y/120 volt electrical system. What MINIMUM size 75°C copper conductors are required for the ungrounded (phase) feeder conductors for this kitchen addition?

    A. 3/0 AWG
    B. 2/0 AWG
    C. 1/0 AWG
    D. 1 AWG

22. When sizing the ungrounded service-entrance conductors for an apartment complex, the MINIMUM demand load, in kW, for ten (10) electric ranges rated at 8 kW each is _____, when applying the general method of load calculations for dwellings.

    A. 27.2 kW
    B. 34.0 kW
    C. 28.2 kW
    D. none of these

23. When exceptions are not to be applied, what MAXIMUM listed standard size dual-element fuses are required for short-circuit, branch-circuit and ground-fault protection for a continuous-duty, 2 hp, single-phase 208 volt motor?

    A. 30 ampere
    B. 35 ampere
    C. 25 ampere
    D. 20 ampere

24. Determine the MAXIMUM number of 125-volt, general-purpose, duplex receptacles, the NEC® permits to be protected by a 20-ampere, 120 volt, single-pole circuit breaker in an office building.

    A. eighteen
    B. fifteen
    C. thirteen
    D. ten

25. The MAXIMUM allowable ampacity of a size 6 AWG XHHW aluminum conductor when there are not more than three (3) conductors installed in a conduit in a wet location, where the expected ambient temperature will reach 100°F, is _____.

    A. 44.0 amperes
    B. 50.0 amperes
    C. 52.8 amperes
    D. 57.2 amperes

26. Given: In a residential kitchen you are supplying a 6 kW cooktop, a 5 kW oven and a 6 kW oven from a single branch-circuit. Determine the MINIMUM branch-circuit demand load, in kW, as per the NEC®.

    A. 17.0 kW
    B. 9.35 kW
    C. 11.9 kW
    D. 10.0 kW

27. Determine the approximate voltage drop on a single-phase, 240-volt branch-circuit, supplying a 42 ampere load with size 6 AWG THWN-2 copper conductors, a distance of 125 feet from the panelboard.
(K = 12.9)

    A. 5 volts
    B. 7 volts
    C. 9 volts
    D. 11 volts

28. Disregarding exceptions, the MAXIMUM number of 3/0 AWG THWN copper conductors the NEC® permits to be installed in a 4 inch x 4 inch x 4 feet metal wireway is _____.

    A. thirty
    B. ten
    C. eleven
    D. twelve

29. A junction box is used for a 90° angle pull where eight (8) size 4 AWG THW copper conductors enter the box in a trade size 1½ in. EMT and leave the box in a trade size 2 in. EMT. The conductors are not required to be spliced. Disregarding exceptions, the MINIMUM size of the pull box as required by the NEC® is _____.

    A. 9 in. x 9 in.
    B. 12 in. x 12 in.
    C. 9 in. x 12 in.
    D. 12 in. x 18 in.

30. Fifty (50) feet of multioutlet assembly are to be installed in a continuous length in an office occupancy. Office equipment and appliances supplied from the multioutlet assembly are likely to be used simultaneously. How many 20-ampere, 120-volt circuits are needed to supply the multioutlet assembly?

    A. five
    B. four
    C. three
    D. two

31. According to the NEC®, the full-load running current of a 50 hp, 480 volt, 3-phase, synchronous-type motor with a 90 percent power factor is _____.

    A. 52.0 amperes
    B. 65.0 amperes
    C. 71.5 amperes
    D. 57.2 amperes

32. Given: Four (4) size 2/0 AWG conductors contained in a 2 in. conduit enter a pull-box on the "east" side. The conductors then make a U turn in the box and go out a 2½ in. conduit on the same side. What is the MINIMUM distance required from the "east" side of the box to the opposite, "west" side, in inches?

    A. 12 inches
    B. 15 inches
    C. 17 inches
    D. 20 inches

33. Disregarding all exceptions, what is the largest inverse time circuit breaker allowed to provide short-circuit, branch-circuit and ground-fault protection for a 5 hp, 230-volt, single-phase continuous-duty motor?

    A. 30 amperes
    B. 40 amperes
    C. 60 amperes
    D. 70 amperes

34. A retail store building measures 60 ft. by 80 ft. and has a 208Y/120 volt electrical system; the building has sixty (60) linear feet of show window lighting. Disregarding exceptions, determine the MINIMUM number of 20-ampere, 120-volt branch-circuits the NEC® requires for the continuous-duty show window and general lighting for the store.

    A. eleven
    B. twelve
    C. thirteen
    D. fourteen

35. What is the approximate horsepower rating of a 3-phase, 208-volt motor that draws 21 amperes, has a 87 percent power factor and is 70 percent efficient?

    A. 8 hp
    B. 4 hp
    C. 6 hp
    D. 10 hp

36. A three-phase transformer having a 480Y/277 volt primary and a 208Y/120 volt secondary is used to supply a balanced 120-volt, single-phase lighting load of 50,000 VA. What load, does the lighting load add to the ungrounded conductors on the primary side of the transformer?

    A. 180 amperes
    B. 104 amperes
    C. 156 amperes
    D. 60 amperes

37. If overcurrent protection is not required on the secondary side of a transformer having a 480Y/277 volt primary, with a primary current of 100 amperes, the rating of the primary overcurrent device should not exceed _____.

    A. 100 amperes
    B. 250 amperes
    C. 125 amperes
    D. 200 amperes

38. A 240-volt, 20-ampere, single-phase circuit is permitted to serve a MAXIMUM of _____ of residential baseboard heating.

    A. 3,840 watts
    B. 2,400 watts
    C. 90 watts
    D. 135 watts

39. Determine the general lighting and general-use receptacle demand load, in VA, for the guest rooms of a twenty-four (24) unit motel. Each guest room has 600 square feet of living area.

    A. 14,400 VA
    B. 13,520 VA
    C. 21,600 VA
    D. 28,800 VA

40. A metal device box to be installed will contain the following:

    - 1 device
    - 2 cable clamps
    - 2 spliced grounding conductors

    To allow for the conductors, clamps and device the MAXIMUM number of conductors permitted in the box must be reduced by _____ conductors.

    A. one
    B. two
    C. three
    D. four

41. A commercial building with a 3-wire, 120/240 volt, single-phase service has a total load of 48,000 VA after all demand factors have been considered. The ungrounded service-entrance conductors shall have a MINIMUM ampacity of _____.

    A. 200 amperes
    B. 150 amperes
    C. 400 amperes
    D. 300 amperes

42. Determine the ampacity of a size 2/0 AWG THW aluminum conductor, when four (4) of them are pulled into a 15 foot long conduit? All conductors are current-carrying and the ambient temperature is 50°C.

    A. 81 amperes
    B. 105 amperes
    C. 108 amperes
    D. 140 amperes

43. Disregarding exceptions, the ampacity of the phase conductors from the terminals of a 25 kW, 240-volt, single-phase generator to the first overcurrent device protecting the load shall be at LEAST _____.

    A. 104 amperes
    B. 120 amperes
    C. 130 amperes
    D. 83 amperes

44. Determine the MINIMUM size ladder type cable tray width required for the following combination of listed single conductors, rated 600 volts, to be installed in the cable tray:

    - eight – size 750 kcmil THWN
    - six – size 500 kcmil THWN

    A. 12 inches
    B. 18 inches
    C. 24 inches
    D. 30 inches

45. What is the MINIMUM standard current rating of a circuit breaker that may be used as the disconnecting means for a 50 hp, 480-volt, 3-phase, continuous-duty, induction type motor as permitted by the NEC®?

    A. 175 amperes
    B. 150 amperes
    C. 80 amperes
    D. 75 amperes

46. Disregarding exceptions, the MAXIMUM continuous load, in VA, permitted to be connected to a 40-ampere rated, 240-volt, single-phase branch-circuit is _____.

    A. 7,680 VA
    B. 12,000 VA
    C. 4,800 VA
    D. 9,600 VA

47. A 9.6 kVA, 240-volt, single-phase non-continuous load will be located ninety (90) feet from the panelboard. Where the voltage drop is to be limited to 3 percent, what MINIMUM size copper branch-circuit conductors are required to supply the load? (K = 12.9)

    A. 6 AWG
    B. 2 AWG
    C. 8 AWG
    D. 10 AWG

48. What MINIMUM size 75°C copper branch-circuit conductors are required to supply a 208-volt, 3-phase, 30 horsepower motor with a nameplate current rating of 80 amperes, used in a continuous duty application?

    A. 2 AWG
    B. 3 AWG
    C. 4 AWG
    D. 6 AWG

49. A 120-volt residential ceiling fan draws 2.5 amperes of current and is operated for an average of 8 hours per day. What would it cost to operate the fan for 30 days at 9 cents per kWH?

    A. $6.48
    B. $64.48
    C. $0.22
    D. $8.10

50. A metal device box will contain one (1) duplex receptacle, two (2) cable clamps and two (2) size 12/2 AWG with ground nonmetallic sheathed cables. The device box must have a cubic inch volume of at LEAST _____.

    A. 13.50 cubic inches
    B. 15.75 cubic inches
    C. 16.00 cubic inches
    D. 18.00 cubic inches

51. What is the approximate FLA primary rating of a 150 kVA, 480Y/277 volt, 3-phase transformer with a 208Y/120 volt secondary?

    A. 542 amperes
    B. 313 amperes
    C. 365 amperes
    D. 181 amperes

52. Where the transformer in the previous question is installed for a commercial installation, what demand load, in amperes, would sixty (60), 125-volt duplex receptacles installed and balanced between the phases, add to the ungrounded primary phases?

    A. 12.5 amperes
    B. 15.0 amperes
    C. 20.0 amperes
    D. 27.7 amperes

53. You are to install size 10/3 AWG NM cable that has a diameter of 5/8 in., the bend radius of the cable shall be a MINIMUM of _____.

    A. 3.125 inches
    B. 8.00 inches
    C. 4.375 inches
    D. 5.00 inches

54. Determine the MAXIMUM number of size 4 AWG THHN copper conductors permitted to be installed in a trade size 1½ in. intermediate metal conduit (IMC) nipple 18 inches long.

    A. twelve
    B. fourteen
    C. fifteen
    D. sixteen

55. Given: A trade size 2 in. electrical metallic tubing (EMT) contains four (4) size 1/0 AWG THWN copper conductors; determine the percentage of conduit fill for this installation.

    A. 14 percent
    B. 22 percent
    C. 40 percent
    D. 53 percent

56. A feeder supplying two (2) 208-volt, 3-phase, continuous-duty motors, one (1) 10 hp with a FLA of 28 amperes indicated on the nameplate, and one (1) 7½ hp with a FLA of 22 amperes indicated on the nameplate, shall have a MINIMUM ampacity of _____.

    A. 57 amperes
    B. 62.5 amperes
    C. 62.7 amperes
    D. 67.2 amperes

57. Determine the initial size adjustable overload protection setting required for a 480-volt, 3-phase, continuous-duty, 15 hp motor when given the following related information:

    - Design B
    - Service factor – 1.15
    - Actual nameplate rating – 18 amperes

    A. 22.50 amperes
    B. 21.00 amperes
    C. 26.25 amperes
    D. 29.60 amperes

58. The NEC® requires the MINIMUM ampacity of branch-circuit conductors that serve a space heating load of 32 amperes to be _____.

    A. 30 amperes
    B. 32 amperes
    C. 35 amperes
    D. 40 amperes

59. Given: A raceway will contain two (2) sets of 208Y/120 volt, 3-phase, 4-wire, branch-circuits. The conductors are to be size 10 AWG THWN copper, serving information technology equipment at an ambient temperature of 30°C. Determine the allowable ampacity of the conductors.

    A. 16.0 amperes
    B. 17.5 amperes
    C. 20.0 amperes
    D. 24.5 amperes

60. Determine the MAXIMUM standard size overcurrent protection device the NEC® permits to protect a 5,000 watt, 240-volt, single-phase water heater, if the overcurrent protection is not marked on the appliance and the branch-circuit conductors are size 6 AWG NM cable.

    A. 30 amperes
    B. 35 amperes
    C. 50 amperes
    D. 40 amperes

61. Determine the general lighting load, in VA, for a two (2) story single-family dwelling unit with outside dimensions of 60 feet by 125 feet.

    A. 7,500 VA
    B. 15,000 VA
    C. 22,500 VA
    D. 45,000 VA

62. What is the rated secondary current of a 600 VA single-phase transformer at unity power factor that has a 200 volt input and a 15 volt secondary?

    A. 20 amperes
    B. 400 amperes
    C. 200 amperes
    D. 40 amperes

63. Disregarding exceptions, what is the demand load, in VA, for 120 feet of lighting track installed in a retail outlet when used continuously for display lighting during the business day?

    A. 22,500 VA
    B. 9,000 VA
    C. 11,250 VA
    D. 13,500 VA

64. The MINIMUM size NM cable the NEC® requires for branch-circuit conductors serving a 14 kW, 240-volt, single-phase, residential electric range is _____.

    A. 10 AWG
    B. 6 AWG
    C. 8 AWG
    D. 4 AWG

65. Determine the MINIMUM size 75°C rated conductors permitted to supply a 25 hp, 208-volt, 3-phase, Design C fire pump motor.

    A. 4 AWG
    B. 3 AWG
    C. 2 AWG
    D. 1 AWG

66. Refer to the previous question. Determine the MAXIMUM standard size overcurrent protection device the NEC® permits to protect the fire pump.

    A. 200 amperes
    B. 250 amperes
    C. 350 amperes
    D. 450 amperes

67. Determine the MINIMUM trade size Schedule 40 rigid PVC conduit, longer than 24 inches, required to contain the following copper conductors:

    - three – size 4 AWG THWN-2
    - one – size 8 AWG bare stranded

    A. 1 in.
    B. 1¼ in.
    C. 1½ in.
    D. 2 in.

68. What is the connected load, in VA, of four (4) three-phase, 480-volt air compressors rated at 24.5 amperes each, that are installed at a tire shop?

    A. 47,040 VA
    B. 81,473 VA
    C. 101,841 VA
    D. 65,178 VA

69. Determine the MAXIMUM permitted operational setting of an adjustable inverse time circuit breaker used for branch-circuit, short-circuit and ground-fault protection of a 10 hp, 208-volt, squirrel cage, Design C, continuous-duty motor. Assume no exceptions are to be applied.

    A. 30.8 amperes
    B. 35.7 amperes
    C. 77.0 amperes
    D. 338.0 amperes

70. What MINIMUM size 75°C rated copper branch-circuit conductors are required to supply a 9.0 kW, 208-volt, single-phase storage-type commercial electric water heater?

    A. 10 AWG
    B. 8 AWG
    C. 6 AWG
    D. 4 AWG

71. What is the MINIMUM bend radius for 1 inch diameter corrugated sheath Type MC cable?

    A. 10 inches
    B. 12 inches
    C. 15 inches
    D. 7 inches

72. What MAXIMUM balanced demand load, in VA, is permitted to be connected to a new service of a commercial building, given the following conditions?

    - The service is 208Y/120 volts, three-phase, with a 600-ampere rated main circuit breaker.
    - The service is supplied with two (2) trade size 3½ in. rigid metal conduits, each containing four (4) size 350 kcmil copper conductors with THWN insulation.
    - The MAXIMUM load must not exceed 80% of the ampere rating of the main circuit breaker.

    A. 57,600 VA
    B. 99,840 VA
    C. 172,923 VA
    D. 178,692 VA

Copyright 2016   BrownTechnical.org

73. After all demand factors are taken into consideration for a one-family dwelling having a 120/240 volt, single-phase electrical system, the demand load is determined to be 60,000 VA. What MINIMUM size aluminum THWN conductors are required for the ungrounded (line) service entrance conductors?

    A. 4/0 AWG
    B. 350 kcmil
    C. 400 kcmil
    D. 300 kcmil

74. An individual ac transformer arc welder is to be installed for 240-volt operational voltage. The arc welder is rated 20 amperes primary current, with a duty cycle of 70 percent. The branch-circuit conductors to supply this welder must have a calculated current-carrying capacity of at LEAST _____.

    A. 14 amperes
    B. 17 amperes
    C. 20 amperes
    D. 25 amperes

75. Given: A feeder supplies a continuous load of 240 amperes. In general, the overcurrent protection device protecting this circuit shall have a MINIMUM rating of _____.

    A. 240 amperes
    B. 300 amperes
    C. 250 amperes
    D. 275 amperes

76. Eighteen (18) size 250 kcmil THHW copper conductors are to be installed in a rigid metal conduit (RMC) that is 21 inches long. Determine the MINIMUM standard trade size conduit permitted to enclose the conductors.

    A. 4 in.
    B. 4½ in.
    C. 5 in.
    D. 6 in.

77. When applying the optional method of load calculation for multifamily dwellings, what is the demand, in VA, on the ungrounded service-entrance conductors, of four (4), 8 kW, 240-volt, single-phase, 60 gallon storage type water heaters installed in the common laundry room?

    A. 22,400 VA
    B. 32,000 VA
    C. 24,000 VA
    D. 17,000 VA

78. Where a 200-ampere rated 208Y/120 volt, 4-wire, three-phase service is installed for a commercial occupancy in an area where the ambient temperature reaches 115°F, what MINIMUM size type THWN copper conductors are required for the ungrounded (phase) service-entrance conductors? Consider all conductors to be current-carrying.

    A. 300 kcmil
    B. 250 kcmil
    C. 4/0 AWG
    D. 400 kcmil

79. Disregarding exceptions, what is the demand load, in VA, for fifty (50), 120-volt fluorescent luminaires (light fixtures) installed in an office building, where the luminaire ballast are rated 1.5 amperes each and operated for at least 8 hours per day?

    A. 9,000 VA
    B. 11,250 VA
    C. 12,110 VA
    D. 18,474 VA

80. A one-family dwelling to be built will have 4,000 square feet of livable space, a 600 square foot garage, a 400 square foot open porch, a 2,000 square foot unfinished basement (adaptable for future use), two (2) small appliance branch-circuits and a laundry branch-circuit. Determine the demand load, in VA, on the ungrounded service-entrance conductors for the general lighting and receptacle loads using the standard method of load calculation for a one-family dwelling.

    A. 9,825 VA
    B. 9,125 VA
    C. 22,500 VA
    D. 7,725 VA

81. Given: A metal junction box has a volume of 27 cubic inches and contains a total of six (6) size 12 AWG wires. Additional size 10 AWG conductors are needed to be added to the box. No grounding conductors, devices or fittings are contained in the box. What is the MAXIMUM number of size 10 AWG conductors that may be added to this junction box?

    A. two
    B. five
    C. six
    D. eight

82. An individual ac transformer arc welder is to be installed for 240-volt operational voltage. The arc welder is rated 50 amperes primary current, with a duty cycle of 60 percent. The overcurrent device protecting this welder shall have a MAXIMUM standard rating of _____.

    A. 50 amperes
    B. 60 amperes
    C. 70 amperes
    D. 100 amperes

83. Given: A size 6 AWG NM cable has an ampacity of 55 amperes and is protected with a 50-ampere circuit breaker. In general, the MAXIMUM continuous load, in amperes, the NM cable may supply is _____.

    A. 40 amperes
    B. 44 amperes
    C. 50 amperes
    D. 55 amperes

84. Given: A 75 foot long, trade size 1 in. rigid metal conduit (RMC) contains three (3) size 8 AWG THWN copper conductors. How many size 10 AWG THWN copper conductors may be added in the conduit?

    A. none
    B. ten
    C. eleven
    D. seven

85. What is the MAXIMUM number of size 4/0 AWG XHHW copper conductors permitted to be installed in a trade size 3 in. intermediate metal conduit (IMC) that is one (1) foot long?

    A. twelve
    B. thirteen
    C. fourteen
    D. fifteen

86. Given: A commercial load is supplied from a 3-phase transformer that has a 480Y/277 volt primary and a 208Y/120 volt secondary. The loads on the secondary conductors are as follows:

    - phase A – 7,200 VA
    - phase B – 8,400 VA
    - phase C – 9,600 VA

    Determine the load, in amperes, on phase C on the primary side of the transformer.

    A. 35 amperes
    B. 20 amperes
    C. 12 amperes
    D. 27 amperes

87. How many 20-ampere, 120-volt branch-circuits are needed for general lighting and general-purpose receptacles for a two (2) story office building with outside dimensions of 100 feet x 200 feet with an unknown receptacle load? Circuit breakers of this size are not rated for continuous use.

    A. one-hundred and twenty
    B. sixty
    C. forty
    D. ninety

88. Given: A 120/240 volt, single-phase feeder is to supply a noncontinuous load of 15,300 VA and a continuous load of 18,560 VA. What MINIMUM size 75°C copper feeder conductors are required?

    A. 1/0 AWG
    B. 2/0 AWG
    C. 3/0 AWG
    D. 4/0 AWG

89. An office building contains 180 general-purpose, 125-volt, duplex receptacles rated at 15-amperes each and 20, 125-volt, single receptacles rated at 20-amperes each. What is the demand load, in VA, for the receptacles?

    A. 36,000 VA
    B. 360,000 VA
    C. 23,000 VA
    D. 48,000 VA

90. A 208Y/120 volt electrical system has three (3) separate 1,800 VA lighting loads, the loads are balanced between the phases; and a three-phase 208-volt 7,206 VA motor load. What is the current on the ungrounded conductors supplying this load?

    A. 15 amperes
    B. 20 amperes
    C. 35 amperes
    D. 43 amperes

91. The MINIMUM required size copper grounding electrode conductor connected to the concrete-encased reinforcing steel used as the grounding electrode system for an ac service supplied with three (3) paralleled sets of size 400 kcmil aluminum ungrounded (phase) conductors is _____.

    A. 1 AWG
    B. 3 AWG
    C. 2/0 AWG
    D. 4/0 AWG

92. Determine the MAXIMUM size overload protection permitted for a 480 volt, 3-phase, 15 hp, continuous-duty motor given the following related information:

    - Design B
    - Temperature rise – 44° C
    - Nameplate FLA – 18 amperes

    A. 22.5 amperes
    B. 20.7 amperes
    C. 25.2 amperes
    D. 23.4 amperes

93. A commercial catering service has the following 208-volt, 3-phase intermittent use equipment installed in the kitchen:

    - two – 10 kW ovens
    - one – 3.5 kW fryer
    - one – 4 kW booster heater
    - one – 2.5 kW dishwasher
    - one – 3 kW sterilizer

    The demand, in amperes on the ungrounded service-entrance conductors for this equipment would be _____.

    A. 60 amperes
    B. 92 amperes
    C. 56 amperes
    D. 64 amperes

94. A 200,000 square foot retail discount store is provided with a 480Y/277 volt, 3-phase electrical system from the local utility company. The general lighting for the store is fluorescent, rated 277-volts. Determine the MINIMUM number of 20-ampere, 277-volt, single-phase general lighting branch-circuits needed for the store. Exceptions will not apply.

    A. 108
    B. 136
    C. 250
    D. 68

95. What is the MINIMUM copper conductor size permitted by the NEC®, for a NM cable supplying a 240-volt, single-phase, 8 kW residential cooktop.

    A. 12 AWG
    B. 10 AWG
    C. 8 AWG
    D. 6 AWG

96. Size 12 AWG THW copper conductors are used to supply a 10 ampere, 120-volt, single-phase load. Where voltage drop is to be limited to 3 percent and the K factor is 12.9, determine the approximate MAXIMUM distance the load may be located from the panelboard, when using the size 12 AWG conductors.

    A. 90 feet
    B. 150 feet
    C. 125 feet
    D. 180 feet

97. The allowable ampacity of a size 750 kcmil XHHW aluminum conductor when there are six (6) current-carrying conductors in the raceway, installed in a dry location, where the ambient temperature will reach 22°C is _____.

    A. 323.40 amperes
    B. 365.40 amperes
    C. 361.92 amperes
    D. 348.00 amperes

98. What is the total calculated load, in amperes, of an installation of fifty (50) feet of a 120-volt multioutlet assembly, installed in a continuous length in an office? Assume the outlets are unlikely to be used simultaneously.

    A. 12 amperes
    B. 15 amperes
    C. 19 amperes
    D. 20 amperes

99. Determine the MINIMUM required ampacity of the conductors supplying an elevator motor where given the following related information:

- 5 hp – 208-volts, 3-phase
- 15 minute rated
- nameplate current rating – 18 amperes

    A. 15.3 amperes
    B. 16.2 amperes
    C. 18.0 amperes
    D. 22.5 amperes

100. Determine the MAXIMUM ampere rating for an overload protective device responsive to motor current as permitted by the NEC® used to protect a 20 hp, 230-volt, 3-phase induction type, continuous-duty motor, with FLA of 54 amperes and a temperature rise of 46°C marked on the nameplate. Assume the setting you select will be sufficient to start the motor and modification of this value is not required.

    A. 54.0 amperes
    B. 62.1 amperes
    C. 78.2 amperes
    D. 92.0 amperes

END OF FINAL EXAM

PRACTICE CALCULATIONS EXAMS
EXAM 1
SOLUTIONS

ANSWER	REFERENCE	NEC PG. #
1. D	314.16(B)(2),(4)&(5)	178

    device = 2 conductors
    2 clamps = 1 conductor
    1 bonding jumper = 0 conductors
    2 grounding conductors = 1 conductor
                 TOTAL = 4 conductors

2. D   Ohms Law

$$R = \frac{Volts}{Current} \quad R = \frac{240 \text{ volts}}{20 \text{ amps}} = 12 \text{ ohms resistance}$$

3. B   Current Formula

$$I = \frac{Power}{Volts} \quad I = \frac{1,500 \text{ watts}}{240 \text{ volts}} = 6.25 \text{ amperes}$$

4. C	Tbl. 310.15(B)(16)	154
	Tbl. 310.15(B)(3)(a)	152

Size 4 AWG THWN ampacity (before derating) = 85 amperes
85 amperes x .8 (adjustment factor) = 68 amperes

5. A   Current Formula

$$I = \frac{P}{E} \quad I = \frac{15 \text{ kW} \times 1,000}{208 \text{ volts}} = \frac{15,000}{208} = 72 \text{ amperes}$$

6. C   Current Formula

$$I = \frac{P}{E} \quad I = \frac{kW \times 1,000}{volts} = \frac{150 \times 1,000}{240 \text{ volts}} = \frac{150,000}{240} = 625 \text{ amperes}$$

109

7. C   220.12   61
             Tbl. 220.12   63

2,750 sq. ft. x 3 VA = 8,250 VA (house)
120 volts x 15 amperes = 1,800 VA (one circuit)

$\dfrac{8{,}250 \text{ VA (house)}}{1{,}800 \text{ VA (one circuit)}} = 4.5 = 5$ circuits

8. C   Current Formula

100 watts x 6 luminaires = 600 watts total load

$I = \dfrac{P}{E}$ $I = \dfrac{600 \text{ watts}}{120 \text{ volts}} = 5$ amperes

9. C   430.6(A)(1)   311
              Tbl. 430.250   338
              430.22   316

FLC of 10 hp motor = 30.8 amperes x 125% = 38.5 amperes

10. A   Tbl. 310.15(B)(16)   154
              3-phase current Formula

$I = \dfrac{kVA \times 1{,}000}{E \times 1.732} = \dfrac{40 \times 1{,}000}{208 \text{ volts} \times 1.732} = \dfrac{40{,}000}{360.25} = 111$ amperes

*Note - Size 2 AWG THW conductors with an allowable ampacity of 115 amperes should be selected.

11. A   Tbl. 314.16(B)   179

*Note – Disregard conductor insulation when doing box fill calculations.

Size 12 AWG = 2.25 cu. in. x 4 =   9.00 cubic inches
Size 10 AWG = 2.50 cu. in. x 4 = 10.00 cubic inches
Size 8 AWG = 3.00 cu. in. x 4 = 12.00 cubic inches
                       TOTAL = 31.00 cubic inches

12. D   210.19(A)(1)   52

$\dfrac{20 \text{ amps}}{125\%} = 16$ amperes   or   20 amperes x 80% = 16 amperes

13. B   Current Formula

   I = Power   I = 6,900 VA = 30 amperes
       Volts   230 volts

14. D   440.12(A)(1)   342

   26 amperes x 1.15 = 29.2 amperes

15. A   Tbl. 310.15(B)(16)   154
                          Tbl. 310.15(B)(2)(a)   150

   Size 1/0 AWG THW ampacity (before derating) = 150 amperes
   150 amps x .75 (temperature correction factor) = 112.5 amperes

16. C   Trade Knowledge

   120 volts x 15 amperes = 1800 VA (one circuit)

   11,500 VA (load)   = 6.38 = 7 circuits
   1,800 VA (one circuit

17. B   220.60   65
                          220.82(C)(4)   68

   15,000 VA (heating load) x 65% = 9,750 VA
   *Note – use only the larger of the heating or AC loads

18. C   Current Formula

   I = Watts   I = 1,200 watts = 10 amperes
       Volts   120 volts

19. C   Power Formula

   P = I x E   P = 150 amperes x 240 volts = 36,000 VA

20. A   Tbl. 220.55, Col. B   66

   8.5 kW x 80% = 6.8 kW demand

21. D Tbl. 310.15(B)(16) 154
       Tbl. 310.15(B)(2)(a) 150
       Tbl. 310.15(B)(3)(a) 152

   Size 10 AWG THW ampacity (before derating) = 35 amperes
   35 amperes x .75 (temp. correction) x .8 (adjustment factor) = 21 amperes

22. C 210.19(A)(1), IN #4 53

   120 volts x 3% = 3.6 volts

23. B Chpt. 9, Tbl. 8 721

   VD = $\frac{2KID}{CM}$ = $\frac{2 \times 12.9 \times 45 \text{ amps} \times 175 \text{ ft.}}{26,240 \text{ CM}}$ = $\frac{203,175}{26,240}$ = 7.74 volts dropped

24. C 210.20(A) 53

   $\frac{240 \text{ volts} \times 20 \text{ amps}}{125\%}$ = 3,840 VA

25. C 430.6(A)(1) 311
       Tbl. 430.250 338
       430.22 316
       Tbl. 310.15(B)(16) 154

   FLC of 25 hp motor = 74.8 amperes x 125% = 93.5 amperes

   *Note - Size 3 AWG THWN conductors with an allowable ampacity of 100 amperes should be selected.

PRACTICE CALCULATIONS EXAMS
EXAM 2
SOLUTIONS

ANSWER	REFERENCE	NEC PG.#

1. D   Power Formula

     P = I x E x PF   P = 8 amperes x 115 volts x .8 (PF) = 736 VA

2. A   344.24   206
                 Chpt. 9, Tbl. 2   711

3. D   Chpt. 9, Note 4 to Tbls.   711

4. C   314.28(A)(1)   183

     $\dfrac{12 \text{ in. (box length)}}{8 \text{ (conduit)}}$ = 1.5 or 1½ inches

5. B   220.14(I)   63
                 220.44   64
                 Tbl. 220.44   64

     180 VA x 115 receptacles = 20,700 VA (before demand factors)

     1st 10,000 VA @ 100% =   10,000 VA
     20,700 VA – 10,000 VA = 10,700 VA @ 50% =   5,350 VA
                              DEMAND = 15,350 VA

6. A   220.14(I)   63

     180 VA x 115 receptacles = 20,700 VA (receptacles)
     120 volts x 20 amps = 2,400 VA (one circuit)

     $\dfrac{20,700 \text{ VA (receptacles)}}{2,400 \text{ VA (one circuit)}}$ = 8.625 = 9 circuits

7. D   220.12   61
              Tbl. 220.12   63
              230.42(A)(1)   82
              220.40   64
              Art. 100 Def.   27

   100 ft. x 75 ft. = 7,500 sq. ft. x 3 VA = 22,500 VA x 1.25 = 28,125 VA

8. D   210.19(A)(1)   52
              210.11(A)   51

   $\dfrac{14{,}000 \text{ VA (building)} \times 125\%}{120 \text{ volts} \times 20 \text{ amps (ckt.)}} = \dfrac{17{,}500 \text{ VA}}{2{,}400 \text{ VA}} = 7.29 = 8 \text{ circuits}$

   *Note – Branch-circuits need only to supply the actual connected load.

9. D   Art. 100 Def.   27
              220.40   64
              220.14(G)(2)   62
              230.42(A)(1)   82

   50 ft. x 200 VA = 10,000 VA x 125% = 12,500 VA

10. A   see above

    Receptacles   = 15,350 VA
    General lighting   = 28,125 VA
    Show window lighting = 12,500 VA
         TOTAL   = 55,975 VA

11. D   Ohms Law

    Resistance = $\dfrac{4 \text{ ohms}}{1{,}000 \text{ ft.}}$ = .004 ohms per ft.

    .004 ohms x 300 ft. = 1.2 ohms total resistance

    VD = I x R   VD = 5 amperes x 1.2 ohms = 6 volts dropped

12. B   Chpt. 9, Tbl. 5   718

    4/0 AWG THWN = .3237 sq. in. x 3 = .9711 square inches
    2/0 AWG THWN = .2223 sq. in. x 3 = .6669 square inches
                    TOTAL= 1.6380 square inches

114

13. C   Ohms Law

.004 ohms + .004 ohms = .008 ohms total resistance

I = E   I = 120 volts   = 15,000 amperes
    R   .008 ohms

14. D   Tbl. 220.56   67
                                 Current Formula

   5.0 kVA
   3.5 kVA
   9.0 kVA
17.5 kVA x 90% (demand) = 15.75 kVA

I = Power   I = 15.75 kVA x 1,000 = 15,750 = 65.525 amperes
    Volts   240 volts   240

15. C   Current Formula

I = P   I = 15 kVA x 1,000 = 15,000 VA = 62.5 amperes
    E   240 volts   240 volts

16. C   450.3(B)   348
                                 Tbl. 450.3(B) & Note 1   349
                                 Current Formula
                                 240.6(A)   91

I = 20 kVA x 1,000 = 20,000 = 41.66 amps x 125% = 52.07 amperes
    480 volts   480

*Note – The next standard size fuses with a rating of 60 amperes should be selected.

17. A   Current Formula

I = hp x 746 watts
    E x Eff. x PF

I = 10 hp x 746 watts   = 7,460 = 46.88 amperes
    208 volts x .9 x .85 159.12

18. D   Tbl. 352.44   210

4.06 (length change per 100 ft.) x 2.5 = 10.15 inches

19. C   Chpt. 9, Tbl. 5   717 & 718
                              Chpt. 9, Tbl. 4   712

Size 12 AWG THHN   = .0133 sq. in. x 4 = .0532 square inches
Size 6 AWG THW   = .0726 sq. in. x 3 = .2178 square inches
Size 4 AWG THW   = .0973 sq. in. x 3 = .2919 square inches
Size 2 AWG THW   = .1333 sq. in. x 3 = .3999 square inches
                                    TOTAL = .9629 square inches

*Note – This installation requires a 2 inch EMT @ 40% fill = 1.342 square inches

20. A   Current Formula

$$I = \frac{P}{E \times Eff.} \quad\quad I = \frac{746 \text{ watts} \times 5 \text{ hp}}{240 \text{ volts} \times .75} = \frac{3,730}{180} = 20.7 \text{ amperes}$$

21. C   250.102(D)   119
                                250.122(C)   124
                                Tbl. 250.122   125

22. C   430.6(A)(1)   311
                                Tbl. 430.250   338
                                430.24(1)&(2)   318

10 hp FLC = 30.8 amps x 125% = 38.5 amperes
7½ hp FLC = 24.2 amps x 100% = 24.2 amperes
                           TOTAL = 62.7 amperes

23. C   220.14(I)   63

120 volts x 20 amperes = 2,400 VA (breaker)

$$\frac{2,400 \text{ VA (breaker)}}{180 \text{ VA (receptacle)}} = 13 \text{ receptacles}$$

24. D   314.16   178
                                314.16(B)(1),(2) & (4)   178
                                Tbl. 314.16(B)   179

#12 THHN   = 2.25 cu. in. x 6 = 13.5   cubic inches
3-way switch = 2 #12 wires = 2.25 cu. in. x 2 = 4.5   cubic inches
2 clamps = 1 #12 wire   = 2.25 cu. in. x 1 = 2.25 cubic inches
                                              TOTAL = 20.25 cubic inches

*Note – This would require the box listed at 21 cubic inches.

25. A   3-Phase Current Formula

$$I = \frac{kVA \times 1{,}000}{E \times 1.732} = \frac{36 \times 1{,}000}{208 \times 1.732} = \frac{36{,}000}{360.25} = 99.9 \text{ amperes}$$

PRACTICE CALCULATIONS EXAMS
EXAM 3
SOLUTIONS

ANSWER	REFERENCE	NEC PG.#
1. A	220.53	65

4,800 VA
1,200 VA
1,150 VA
   800 VA
<u>1,200 VA</u>
9,150 VA x 75% (demand) = 6,862.5 VA

2. D	220.61(B)(1)	67
3. C	Current Formula	153
Tbl. 310.15(B)(7)		

$I = \dfrac{P}{E}$ $I = \dfrac{36,000 \text{ VA}}{240 \text{ volts}} = 150$ amperes

4. C	General Knowledge	

$PF = \dfrac{\text{Watts}}{\text{VA}} = \dfrac{5,000 \text{ watts}}{208 \text{ volts} \times 30 \text{ amps}} = \dfrac{5,000}{6,240} = .80$ or 80%

5. D	230.42(A)(1)	82
	240.4(B)(1),(2)&(3)	90
	240.6(A)	91
	Current Formula	

Continuous load = 16,200 VA x 125% = 20,250 VA
Noncontinuous load   = <u>12,200 VA</u>
                                 TOTAL = 32,450 VA

6. C	220.54	65
	Tbl. 220.54	65

5.5 kW x 6 = 33 kW x 75% (demand) = 24.75 kW x 1,000 = 24,750 watts

7. A   392.22(A)(3)(a)   241

   24 in. x 90% = 21.6 in. (allowable fill)

   $\dfrac{21.6 \text{ in. (allowable fill)}}{1.5 \text{ in. (cable)}}$ = 14.4 = 14 cables

8. C   630.11(A)   552
                               Tbl. 630.11(A)   552

   40 amps x .78 = 31.2 amperes

9. D   630.12(A)   552
                               240.6(A)   91

   40 amps x 200% = 80 amperes

10. C   220.14(I)   63
                               Current Formula

   10 x 180 VA = 1,800 VA (receptacles)
   6 x 100 VA =   600 VA (luminaires)
        TOTAL = 2,400 VA

   I = $\dfrac{\text{Power}}{\text{Volts}}$ I = $\dfrac{2,400 \text{ VA}}{120 \text{ volts}}$ = 20 amperes

11. D   Chpt. 9, Notes 4 & 7   711
                               Chpt. 9, Tbl. 4   713
                               Chpt. 9, Tbl. 5   719

   3" IMC @ 60% fill = 4.753 square inches (allowable fill)

   $\dfrac{4.753 \text{ sq. in. (allowable fill)}}{.3197 \text{ sq. in. (wire)}}$ = 14.86 = 15 wires

12. B   Chpt. 9, Tbl. 8   721

   CM = $\dfrac{2KID}{VD}$ = $\dfrac{2 \times 12.9 \times 16 \text{ amps} \times 100 \text{ ft.}}{3.6 \text{ volts (3\% of 120 V)}}$ = $\dfrac{41,288}{3.6}$ = 11,467 CM

   *NOTE – Size 8 AWG conductors with a CMA of 16,510 CM should be selected.

13. B   334.80   198
          Tbl. 310.15(B)(16) 154
          310.15(B)(3)(a)   150
          Tbl. 310.15(B)(3)(a) 152

30 amperes x 70% (adjustment factor) = 21 amperes

*NOTE – Under this condition all grounded and ungrounded conductors are considered to be current-carrying. Also, 20 amperes should be selected because, 21 amperes exceeds the allowable ampacity value for 60°C rated conductors of the same size.

14. B   430.6(A)(1)   311
          Tbl. 430.250   338
          Tbl. 430.52   323
          240.6(A)   91

10 hp FLC = 30.8 amperes x 250% = 77 amperes

*NOTE – Because no exceptions apply, go down to the next standard size circuit breaker with a rating of 70 amperes.

15. A   Trade Knowledge
          Current Formula

*NOTE – The voltage to ground on any one of the three phases is 120 volts.

I = P/E = 8,400 VA / 120 volts = 70 amperes

16. C   Chpt. 9, Tbl. 8   721

VD = 2KID/CM = (2 x 12.9 x 20 amps x 150 ft.) / 10,380 CM = 7.45 volts dropped

17. C   General Knowledge

Percentage = 7.45 (VD) / 120 volts (source) = .062 or 6.2%

18. A   Tbl. 314.16(A)   179
          314.16(B)(4)   178

9 Size 12 AWG wires per gang x 3 gang = 27 wires
3 switches (2 wires per switch) = - 6 wires
          TOTAL = 21 wires may be added

19. C   General Knowledge
                               3-phase power Formula

   P = I x E x 1.732 = 150 amperes x 208 volts x 1.732 = 54,038 VA

20. C   Chpt. 9, Note 4 to Tbls.   711
                               Chpt. 9, Tbl. 5   718
                               Chpt. 9, Tbl. 4   714

   Size 3/0 AWG THWN = .2679 sq. in. x 3 = .8037 square inches
   Size 1 AWG   THWN = .1562 sq. in. x 1 = .1562 square inches
   Size 6 AWG   THWN = .0507 sq. in. x 1 = .0507 square inches
                                  TOTAL = 1.0106 square inches

   *NOTE – 1½" rigid @ 60% fill = 1.243 sq. in. should be selected.

21. B   Current Formula

   I = P = 3,500 watts = 14.58 amperes
       E   240 volts

22. C   Tbl. 310.15(B)(16)   154
                               Tbl. 310.15(B)(2)(a)   150

   4/0 AWG THWN ampacity (before derating) = 230 amperes

   230 amperes x .88 (temperature correction factor) = 202.4 amperes

23. D   220.52(A)&(B)   65

   Small appliance circuits   3 x 1,500 VA = 4,500 VA
   Laundry   1 x 1,500 VA = 1,500 VA
                                    TOTAL = 6,000 VA

24. B   Tbl. 220.55, Col. B   66
                               Tbl. 220.55, Note 4   66
                               334.80   198
                               Tbl. 310.15(B)(16)   154
                               Current Formula

   I = watts = 8,000 watts (demand) = 33.3 amperes
       volts   240 volts

   *NOTE – Size 8 AWG NM cable (rated at 60 deg. C.) with an ampacity of 40 amperes should be selected.

25. B   Tbl. 250.66   115

350 kcmil x 2 (parallel conductors) = 700 kcmil

*NOTE – A 1/0 AWG COPPER grounding electrode conductor should be selected.

PRACTICE CALCULATIONS EXAMS
EXAM 4
SOLUTIONS

ANSWER	REFERENCE	NEC PG.#
1. B	430.22(E)	316
	Tbl. 430.22(E)	317
	Tbl. 310.15(B)(16)	154

25 amperes x 120% = 30 amperes

| 2. C | 430.109(C)(2) | 331 |

15 amperes x 80% = 12 amperes

| 3. C | Series Circuit Rules | |

RT = R1 + R2 + R3 + R4

RT = 2 ohms + 4 ohms + 6 ohms + 10 ohms = 22 ohms

| 4. A | Ohms Law | |

$I = \dfrac{E}{R} = \dfrac{240 \text{ volts}}{22 \text{ ohms}} = 10.9$ amperes

| 5. C | 3-phase current Formula | |

$I = \dfrac{kVA \times 1{,}000}{E \times 1.732} = \dfrac{75 \text{ kVA} \times 1{,}000}{208 \times 1.732} = \dfrac{75{,}000}{360.25} = 208.3$ amperes

| 6. C | 450.45(C) | 355 |

150 kVA x 3 sq. in. (per kVA) = 450 square inches

Copyright 2016   BrownTechnical.org

7. C   210.19(A)(1)   52

   300 watts x 125% = 375 watts or VA (demand per luminaire)

   120 volts x 20 amperes = 2,400 VA (circuit)

   $\dfrac{2{,}400\ \text{VA (circuit)}}{375\ \text{VA (luminaire)}}$ = 6.4 or 6 luminaires

8. A   Chpt. 9, Tbl. 5   716 & 717

   Size 14 AWG THW   - .0139 sq. in. x 2 = .0278 square inches
   Size 10 AWG RHW w/o cover - .0333 sq. in. x 10 = .3330 square inches
                                           TOTAL = .3608 square inches

9. A   Chpt. 9, Tbl. 5   718
                            Chpt. 9, Tbl. 4   712

   250 kcmil THWN - 0.3970 sq. in. x 1 = 0.3970 sq. in.
   400 kcmil THWN - 0.5863 sq. in. x 3 = 1.7589 sq. in.
                               Total   = 2.1559 sq. in.

   *NOTE - A trade size 3 in. FMC with a permitted fill area of 2.827 sq. in.
           @ 40% should be selected.

10. A   376.22(A)   230
                            Chpt. 9, Tbl. 5   718

   4" x 4" = 16 sq. in. x 20% = 3.2 square inches (allowable fill)

   $\dfrac{3.2\ \text{sq. in. (allowable fill)}}{.1855\ \text{sq. in. (wire)}}$ = 17.2 = 17 wires

11. C   422.13   292
                            422.10(A)   291
                            Current Formula

   I = $\dfrac{kW \times 1{,}000}{\text{volts}}$ = $\dfrac{9 \times 1{,}000}{240}$ = $\dfrac{9{,}000}{240}$ = 37.5 amperes

   37.5 amperes (load) x 125% = 46.9 amperes

12. B   430.6(A)(2)   312
                            430.32(A)(1)   319

   20 amperes x 115% = 23 amperes

13.	D	430.6(A)(2)	312
		430.32(C)	319

20 amperes x 130% = 26 amperes

14.	D	Current Formula	

$$I = \frac{Power}{Volts} = \frac{600\ VA}{15\ volts} = 40\ amperes$$

*NOTE – The VA rating of a transformer is the same on both primary and secondary.

15.	B	551.71	500

200 sites x 70% = 140 sites with 30-ampere, 125-volt receptacles.

16.	C	314.28(A)(1)	183

2" (raceway) x 8 = 16 inches

17.	B	314.16(B)(1)	178
		Tbl. 314.16(B)	179

Size 12 AWG – 2.25 cu. in. x 4 = 9 cubic inches
Size 10 AWG – 2.50 cu. in. x 4 = <u>10 cubic inches</u>
TOTAL = 19 cubic inches

18.	C	Current Formula	
		Tbl. 310.15(B)(7)	153

$$I = \frac{P}{E} = \frac{48\ kW \times 1{,}000}{240\ volts} = \frac{48{,}000}{240} = 200\ amperes$$

19.	B	430.6(A)(1)	311
		Tbl. 430.248	337
		430.22	316
		Tbl. 310.15(B)(16)	154

5 hp FLC = 30.8 amperes x 125% = 38.5 amperes

*NOTE – The ampacity of the conductors required is based on Tbl. 430.248, NOT the nameplate rating.

20. D   550.31   489
                  Tbl. 550.31   489

16,000 VA x 25 = 400,000 VA x 24% (demand factor) = 96,000 VA

*NOTE – Mobile homes shall be calculated at a MINIMUM of 16,000 VA

21. C   Current Formula

I = $\frac{\text{Power}}{\text{Volts}}$ = $\frac{96,000 \text{ VA}}{240 \text{ volts}}$ = 400 amperes

22. A   Chpt. 9, Tbl. 5   717 & 718
                  Chpt. 9, Tbl. 4   712

Size 10 AWG TW   = .0243 sq. in. x 24 = .5832 square inches
Size 10 AWG THW = .0243 sq. in. x 10 = .2430 square inches
Size 12 AWG THHN = .0133 sq. in. x 14 = .1862 square inches
                              TOTAL = 1.0124 square inches

*NOTE – A trade size 2 in. EMT with an allowable fill of 1.342 sq. in. @ 40% should be selected.

23. D   430.6(A)(1)   311
                  Tbl. 430.250   338
                  430.52(C)(1)Ex.2(c)   322
                  240.6(A)   91

40 hp, 3 ph., 230-volts FLC = 104 amperes x 300% = 312 amperes

*NOTE – In this case you must go down to the next size standard breaker.

24. D   Tbl. 220.42   64

Total lighting equals 205,400 VA
1st 3,000 VA @ 100%   = 3,000 VA
3,001 to 120,000 VA @ 35% = 117,000 VA @ 35%   = 40,950 VA
Remainder 205,400 VA – 120,000 VA = 85,400 VA @ 25%   = 21,350 VA
                                              TOTAL   = 65,300 VA

25. A   Chpt. 9, Tbl. 8   721
                          Current Formula
                          Voltage drop formula

$$VD = \frac{2 \times K \times I \times D}{CM}$$

1st find I $I = \frac{VA}{Volts}$ $\frac{10{,}800 \text{ VA}}{240 \text{ volts}}$ = 45 amperes

$$VD = \frac{2 \times 12.9 \times 45 \text{ amps} \times 200 \text{ ft.}}{26{,}240 \text{ CM}} = \frac{232{,}200}{26{,}240} = 8.84 \text{ volts dropped}$$

PRACTICE CALCULATIONS EXAMS
EXAM 5
SOLUTIONS

ANSWER	REFERENCE	NEC PG.#
1. B	Tbl 310.15(B)(3)(c)	152
2. D	Chpt. 9, Tbl. 8	721

Size 10 AWG uncoated copper = 1.24 ohms per 1,000 feet

$\frac{1.24 \text{ ohms}}{1,000 \text{ ft.}}$ = 0.00124 ohms per ft. x 375 ft. = .465 ohms

3. B	422.11(E)(3)	291
	240.6(A)	91
	Current Formula	

$I = \frac{VA}{Volts}$ $I = \frac{3,600 \text{ VA}}{240 \text{ volts}}$ = 15 amperes

15 amps x 150% = 22.5 amperes

*NOTE – You are permitted to go up to the next standard size circuit breaker which is rated 25 amperes.

4. C	220.12	61
	Tbl. 220.12	63

70 ft. x 30 ft. = 2,100 sq. ft. x 3 VA per sq. ft. = 6,300 VA (house load)

120 volts x 15 amperes = 1,800 VA (one circuit)

$\frac{6,300 \text{ VA (house)}}{1,800 \text{ VA (circuit)}}$ = 3.5 = 4 circuits

5. B	Tbl. 220.55, Col. C	66
	Note 1 to Tbl. 220.55	66

18 kW – 12 kW = 6 kW x 5% = 30% (increase Col. C)

8 kW (one appliance) x 130% = 10.4 kW demand load

6. A   Tbl. 310.15(B)(16)   154

    Size 12 AWG THHN ampacity (before derating) = 30 amperes

    30 amperes x .87 (temperature correction) = 26.1 amperes

7. A   220.14(I)   63
                         220.44   64
                         Tbl. 220.44   64

    75 receptacles x 180 VA ea. = 13,500 VA (before demand factor)

    1st 10,000 VA @ 100% = 10,000 VA
        3,500 VA @ 50% = 1,750 VA
                          11,750 VA (after demand factors)

8. C   Chpt. 9, Tbl. 5   718
                         Chpt. 9, Tbl. 8   721
                         Chpt. 9, Tbl. 4   713

    Size 250 kcmil THWN = .3970 sq. in. x 3 = 1.191 square inches
    Size 2   AWG bare = .0670 sq. in. x 1 = .067 square inches
                                    TOTAL = 1.258 square inches

    *NOTE – A trade size 2 in. IMC with an allowable fill of 1.452 sq. in. @ 40%, should be selected.

9. B   Ohms Law
                         Power Formula

    $R = \dfrac{E}{I}$ $R = \dfrac{240 \text{ volts}}{53 \text{ amps}} = 4.53$ ohms (resistance)

    $I = \dfrac{E}{R}$ $I = \dfrac{208 \text{ volts (source)}}{4.53 \text{ ohms (resistance)}} = 45.9$ amperes

    $P = I \times E = \dfrac{45.9 \text{ amps} \times 208 \text{ volts}}{1,000} = 9,554$ VA = 9.55 kVA

10. D   Tbl. 314.16(B)   179
                         314.28(A)   183

11. A   Tbl. 310.15(B)(16)   154

    $\dfrac{200 \text{ amps (load)}}{.75 \text{ (temp. correction)}} = 266.6$ ampacity required

    *NOTE – This condition requires size 300 kcmil THWN conductors with an allowable ampacity of 285 amperes.

12. C   630.12(A)   552

    75 amperes x 200% = 150 amperes

13. D   314.28(A)(1)   183

    1½ in. (conduit) x 8 = 12 inches

14. A   220.43(B)   64
                  210.19(A)(1)   52

    $\dfrac{200 \text{ feet}}{2 \text{ feet}}$ = 100 x 150 VA = 15,000 VA (track ltg.) x 125% = 18,750

    120 volts x 20 amperes = 2,400 VA (one circuit)

    $\dfrac{18{,}750 \text{ VA (track ltg.)}}{2{,}400 \text{ VA (circuit)}}$ = 7.8 = 8 circuits

15. B   Tbl. 430.250 & *NOTE   338

    FLC of motor = 63 amperes x 1.1 (power factor) = 69.3 amperes

16. B   Ohms Law
                  Current Formula

    $I = \dfrac{P}{E} = \dfrac{1{,}000 \text{ watts}}{240 \text{ volts}}$ = 4.16 amperes

    $R = \dfrac{E}{I} = \dfrac{240 \text{ volts}}{4.16 \text{ amps}}$ = 57.69 ohms resistance

17. D   430.6(A)(2)   312
                  430.32(C)   320

    8.8 amperes x 140% = 12.3 amperes

18. B   220.103   70
                 Tbl. 220.103   70
                 230.23(A)   79
                 240.6(A)   91

1st - 60 amperes @ 100% = 60 amperes
2nd - 60 amperes @ 75% = 45 amperes
3rd - 60 amperes @ 65% = 39 amperes
4th - 60 amperes @ 50% = 30 amperes
5th - 60 amperes @ 50% = 30 amperes
              TOTAL   = 204 amperes

19. B   424.3(B)   296
                 210.19(A)(1)   52

1,750 watts x 24 heaters = 42,000 VA x 125% = 52,500 VA

240 volts x 30 amperes = 7,200 VA (one circuit)

$\dfrac{52,500 \text{ VA (heaters)}}{7,200 \text{ VA (circuit)}}$ = 7.29 or 8 circuits

20. A   Tbl. 220.55, Note 4   66
                 Current Formula
                 334.80   198
                 Tbl. 310.15(B)(16)   154

$I = \dfrac{kW \times 1,000}{240 \text{ volts}} = \dfrac{10 \times 1,000}{240} = \dfrac{10,000}{240} = 41.66 \text{ amperes}$

*NOTE – For ampacity purposes, NM cable is rated at 60°C. Therefore, a size 6 AWG Type NM cable which has an ampacity of 55 amperes should be selected.

21. D   General Knowledge

$\dfrac{208 \text{ volts (source)}}{240 \text{ volts (rating)}}$ = .866 or 87%

22. C   220.54   65
                 Power Formula

P = I x E   P = 30 amperes x 240 volts = 7,200 VA

23. C   430.6(A)(1)   311
                 Tbl. 430.248   337
                 430.52(C)(1)   322
                 Tbl. 430.52   323

FLC of 3/4 hp, 240-volt motor = 6.9 amperes x 300% = 20.7 amperes

24. B   Tbl. 220.55, Col. C   66
                 Notes 1 & 4 to Tbl. 220.55   66
                 334.80   198
                 Tbl. 310.15(B)(16)   154
                 Current Formula

17 kW – 12 kW = 5 kW x 5% = 25% increase in Col. C

8 kW (one appliance) x 125% = 10 kW demand

$I = \dfrac{kW \times 1{,}000}{240 \text{ volts}} = \dfrac{10 \times 1{,}000}{240} = \dfrac{10{,}000}{240} = 41.66$ amperes

Size 6 AWG NM cable ampacity rated at 60°C = 55 amperes

25. B   Tbl. 220.12   63
                 Tbl 220.42   64

24 units x 600 x 2 VA = 28,800 VA

1st 20,000 VA @ 50% = 10,000 VA
8,800 VA   @ 40% = 3,520 VA
          Demand load = 13,520 VA

PRACTICE CALCULATIONS EXAMS
EXAM 6
SOLUTIONS

ANSWER	REFERENCE	NEC PG.#
1. B	630.31(A)(2)	553
	Tbl. 630.31(A)(2)	553
	110.14(C)	36
	Tbl. 310.15(B)(16)	154

50 amperes x .71 (multiplier) = 35.5 required ampacity

*NOTE – Because the circuit breaker is rated 60° C, the 60°C ampacity rating of the conductors must be selected, requiring a size 8 AWG THHN.

2. D	440.22(A)	343
	240.6(A)	91

42 amperes x 225% = 94.5 amperes

3. D	424.3(B)	296
	210.20(A)	53
	240.4(B)(1),(2)&(3)	90
	240.6(A)	91
	Current Formula	

$$I = \frac{kW \times 1{,}000}{volts} \quad I = \frac{18 \times 1{,}000}{240 \text{ volts}} = \frac{18{,}000}{240} = 75 \text{ amperes}$$

75 amperes x 125% = 93.75 amperes

*NOTE – The next larger standard size circuit breaker above 94 amperes is rated 100 amperes and should be selected.

4. B	220.14(I)	63

42 receptacles x 180 VA = 7,560 VA

5. B   Tbl. 314.16(A)   179
                     314.16(B)(1),(2),(4)&(5)   178

    receptacle = 2 conductors
    #14/2 w/g = 3 conductors
    clamps   = 1 conductor
       TOTAL   = 6 conductors in box

     9 * size 14 AWG conductors (permitted in box)
    -6 * existing size 14 AWG conductors in box
     3 * size 14 AWG conductors may be added

6. B   550.31   489
                     Tbl. 550.31   489
                     Current Formula

    22,000 VA x 26 mobile homes = 572,000 VA x 24% (demand) = 137,280 VA

    I = P = 137,280 VA = 572 amperes
        E   240 volts

7. A   430.22(E)   316
                     Tbl. 430.22(E)   317

    18 amperes x 85% = 15.3 amperes

    *NOTE – When sizing conductors for intermittent duty motors, the NAMEPLATE
            rating shall be used.

8. B   Power Factor Formula

    PF = ____watts____ = ____6,500 watts____ = _6,500_ = .82 or 82%
         volts x amps   240 volts x 33 amps   7,920

9. D   Trade Knowledge

    120 volts x 24 amperes = _2,880 VA_ = 2,938.7 VA
                              .98 (eff.)

    2,938.7 VA = 2.94 kVA
      1,000

    *NOTE – A transformer has the same kVA rating on the primary and secondary.

10. C   Power Formula

    P = I x E   P= 200 amperes x 240 volts = 48,000 VA

11. A 210.19(A)(1) 52

1.5 amperes (luminaire) x 125% = 1.875 amperes per luminaire

$$\frac{20 \text{ amperes (circuit)}}{1.875 \text{ amperes (luminaire)}} = 10.6 = 10 \text{ luminaires}$$

12. B 314.16(B)(1),(2),(4)&(5) 178
       Tbl. 314.16(B) 179

14 AWG	= 2.00 cu. in. x 4	= 8.00 cubic inches
12 AWG	= 2.25 cu. in. x 4	= 9.00 cubic inches
equip. grnd.	= 2.25 cu. in. x 1	= 2.25 cubic inches
clamps	= 2.25 cu. in. x 1	= 2.25 cubic inches
recept.	= 2.25 cu. in. x 2	= 4.50 cubic inches
switch	= 2.00 cu. in. x 2	= 4.00 cubic inches
	TOTAL	30.00 cubic inches

COMMENT: Clamps, 1 or more, are counted as equal to the largest wire in the box. **314.16(B)(1)** Equipment grounding conductors, 1 or more, are counted as equal to the largest equipment grounding conductor in the box. **314.16(B)(5)** Devices are counted as equal to two conductors, based on the largest conductor connected to the device. **314.16(B)(4)**

13. A 366.22(A) 223
       Chpt. 9, Tbl. 5 718

3 in. x 3 in. = 9 sq. in. x 20% (fill permitted) = 1.8 square inches

size 1/0 AWG THHN/THWN conductor = .1855 square inches

$$\frac{1.8 \text{ sq. in. (gutter)}}{.1855 \text{ sq. in. (wire)}} = 9.7 = 9 \text{ conductors}$$

14. D Current Formula
       Ohms Law

*NOTE – First, find the current and apply Ohms Law.

$$I = \frac{P}{E} = \frac{100 \text{ watts}}{120 \text{ volts}} = .833 \text{ amperes}$$

$$R = \frac{E}{I} = \frac{120 \text{ volts}}{.833 \text{ amps}} = 144.05 \text{ ohms}$$

15. B 220.12 61
       Tbl. 220.12 63

30 ft. x 70 ft. = 2,100 square feet (total)

20 ft. x 25 ft. = 500 square feet (garage)

2,100 sq. ft. (total) − 500 sq. ft. (garage) = 1,600 square feet

1,600 sq. ft. x 3 VA = 4,800 VA

16. C Chpt. 9, Note 4 to Tbls. 711
       Chpt. 9, Tbl. 4 714
       Chpt. 9, Tbl. 5A 720

5 in. rigid metal conduit @ 60% fill = 12.127 square inches (permitted fill)

$\dfrac{12.127 \text{ sq. in. (permitted fill)}}{.6939 \text{ sq. in. (\#500 THHW AL)}}$ = 17.4 = 17 conductors

17. A 210.23(A)(2) 54

20 amperes (circuit) x 50% = 10 amperes

18. C 310.15(B)(5)(c) 152
       220.61(C)(2) 67

*NOTE − Sect. 220.61 permits a reduction of the neutral capacity under certain conditions. But, it does not permit the reduction of the neutral capacity for the portion of the load consisting of nonlinear loads such as fluorescent lighting.

19. A Tbl. 310.15(B)(16) 154
       Tbl. 310.15(B)(3)(a) 152

#12 THWN = 25 amperes (before derating) x .7 (adj. factor) = 17.5 amperes

20. A Tbl. 220.55 & Note 1 66
       220.61(B)(1) 67
       Current Formula

14 kVA − 12 kVA = 2 kVA x 5% = 10% (increase in Col. C)

8 kVA (1 appl. Col. C) x 110% = 8.8 kVA x 1,000 = 8,800 VA

$I = \dfrac{P}{E}$ $I = \dfrac{8{,}800 \text{ VA}}{240 \text{ volts}}$ = 36.7 amperes x 70% (220.61) = 25.7 amperes

21. B   Chpt. 9, Tbl. 5   717-719
         Chpt. 9, Note 8 to Tbls.   711
         Chpt. 9, Tbl. 8   721
         Chpt. 9, Tbl. 4   714

size 6 AWG THW   = .0726 sq. in. x 2 = .1452 square inches
size 4 AWG THWN = .0824 sq. in. x 3 = .2472 square inches
size 1 AWG XHHW = .1534 sq. in. x 3 = .4602 square inches
size 6 AWG bare = .0270 sq. in. x 1 = .0270 square inches
                            TOTAL   = .8796 square inches

*NOTE – A 2" Sch. 80 PVC with an area of 1.150 @ 40 percent fill is required.

22. D   210.19(A)(1)   52
         600.5(A)   519

120 volts x 1.5 amperes = 180 VA x 80 luminaires = 14,400 VA (bldg. ltg.)

14,400 VA x 125% (cont. load) = 18,000 VA

120 volts x 20 amperes = 2,400 VA (one circuit)

$$\frac{18{,}000\ VA\ (bldg.\ ltg.)}{2{,}400\ VA\ (circuit)} = 7.5 = 8\ lighting\ circuits$$

8 lighting circuits + 2 sign circuits = 10 total circuits

23. D   430.72(A)   326
         430.72(B)(2)   326
         Tbl. 430.72(B), Col. C 327

24. B   430.62(A)   325

150 amperes + 50 amperes = 200 amperes

25. C   220.55   65
         Tbl. 220.55, Notes 1&4   66
         Tbl. 220.55, Col. C   66
         Current Formula

4 kVA + 4 kVA + 5 kVA = 13 kVA
13 kVA – 12 kVA = 1 x 5% = 5% increase in Col. C (Note 1)
8 kVA x 1.05% = 8.4 kVA x 1,000 = 8,400 VA

$$I = \frac{VA}{volts} = \frac{8{,}400\ VA}{240\ volts} = 35\ amperes$$

*NOTE – Treat as equivalent to one range (Note 4)

PRACTICE CALCULATIONS EXAMS
EXAM 7
SOLUTIONS

ANSWER	REFERENCE	NEC PG.#

1. D   3-phase power Formula

P = I x E 1.732   P = 800 amperes x 480 volts x 1.732 = 665,088 VA

2. C   210.19(A)(1)   52

.83 ampere (one luminaire) x 125% = 1.0375 amperes

20 amperes (circuit) /1.0375 amperes (luminaire) = 19.27 = 19 luminaires

3. A   314.16(B),(1),(4)&(5)   178
                          Tbl. 314.16(B)   179

3 – size 12 AWG = 2.25 cu. in. x 3 = 6.75 cubic inches
2 – size 14 AWG = 2.00 cu. in. x 2 = 4.00 cubic inches
receptacle   = 2.25 cu. in. x 2 = 4.50 cubic inches
switch   = 2.00 cu. in. x 2 = 4.00 cubic inches
clamps   = 2.25 cu. in. x 1 = 2.25 cubic inches
                                     TOTAL   21.50 cubic inches

4. C   Tbl. 352.44   210

- 10° F to 110° F = 120° total temperature change

5. B   3-phase power Formula
                          3-phase current Formula

P = I x E x 1.732   P = 225 amps x 208 volts x 1.732 = 81,058 VA

*NOTE – The VA rating of a transformer is the same on the primary side as on the secondary side.

I = $\dfrac{VA}{E \times 1.732}$ = $\dfrac{81,058 \text{ VA}}{480 \text{ volts} \times 1.732}$ = $\dfrac{81,058}{831.36}$ = 97.5 amperes

138

6. A   220.56   65
                      Tbl. 220.56   67

ovens -   2 x 20 kW = 40 kW
cooktops -   4 x 15 kW = 60 kW
dishwashers -   2 x 5 kW = 10 kW
water heater -   1 x 9 kW = 9 kW
booster heaters - 2 x 5 kW = 10 kW
                 TOTAL = 129 kW x 65% (demand factor) = 83.85 kW

7. A   220.12   61
                      Tbl. 220.12   63
                      220.52(A)&(B)   65
                      Tbl. 220.42   64

2,400 sq. ft. + 800 sq. ft. = 3,200 sq. ft. x 3 VA = 9,600 VA
two small appliance circuits @ 1,500 VA each   = 3,000 VA
one laundry circuit @ 1,500 VA   = 1,500 VA
         TOTAL CONNECTED LOAD   =14,100 VA

1st 3,000 VA @ 100%   = 3,000 VA
14,100 VA – 3,000 VA = 11,100 VA (remainder) @ 35% = 8,885 VA
                     TOTAL DEMAND LOAD   = 6,885 VA

8. B   445.13   347
                      Current Formula

15 kVA x 1,000 = 15,000 VA

$I = \dfrac{P}{E}$ $I = \dfrac{15,000 \text{ VA}}{240 \text{ volts}} = 62.5$ amperes x 115% = 71.8 amperes

9. D   430.6(A)(1)   311
                      Tbl. 430.250   338

60 hp, 480-volt, 3-phase motor FLC = 61 amperes x 1.1 (pf) = 67.1 amperes

10. C   Fault Current Formula

$I = \dfrac{P}{E \times 1.732} = \dfrac{150,000}{208 \times 1.732} = \dfrac{150,000}{360.25} = 416$ amperes (transformer FLA)

$I_{sca} = \dfrac{\text{transformer FLA}}{\text{transformer impedance}} = \dfrac{416 \text{ amperes}}{2\%} = 20,800$ ASC

11. B   Chpt. 9, Tbl. 8   721

$$CM = \frac{2 \times K \times I \times D}{VD \text{ (permitted)}} = \frac{2 \times 12.9 \times 24 \text{ amps} \times 150 \text{ ft.}}{7 \text{ volts}} = 13,268 \text{ CM}$$

Size 8 AWG THWN conductors with a CMA of 16,510 should be selected.

12. C   Art. 100 Def.   27
                    220.43(A)   64
                    220.14(G)(2)   62
                    210.19(A)(1)   52

200 VA x 120 ft. (show window) = 24,000 VA x 125% = 30,000 VA

120 volts x 20 amperes = 2,400 VA (one circuit)

$$\frac{30,000 \text{ VA (load)}}{2,400 \text{ VA (circuit)}} = 12.5 = 13 \text{ circuits required}$$

13. A   430.6(A)(2)   312
                    430.32(C)   320

20 amperes x 130% = 26 amperes

14. D   General Knowledge

200 watts (light) x 8 hrs. = 1,600 watt hours / 1,000 = 1.6 kWH
1.6 kWH x $0.09 = $0.144

15. B   430.6(A)(1)   311
                    Tbl. 430.250   338
                    430.110(A)   332
                    240.4(B)(1), (2) & (3) 90
                    240.6(A)   91

40 hp, 208-V, 3-phase motor FLC = 114 amperes x 115% = 131.1 amperes

*NOTE – The next standard size circuit breaker with a rating of 150 amperes should be selected.

16. A   220.12   61
                    Tbl. 220.12   63
                    220.14(K)(2)   63
                    230.42(A)(2)   82

225 ft. x 90 ft. = 20,250 sq. ft. x 10 stories = 202,500 sq. ft. total

202,500 sq. ft. x 4.5 VA = 911,250 VA

17. D   Tbl. 220.12   63
        210.20(A)   53

202,500 sq. ft. x 3.5 VA = 708,750 VA x 125% = 885,938 VA

277 volts x 20 amperes = 5,540 VA (one circuit)

$\dfrac{885{,}938 \text{ VA (bldg.)}}{5{,}540 \text{ VA (circuit)}}$ = 160 lighting circuits

18. D   430.6(A)(1)   311
        Tbl. 430.250   338
        430.22   316
        110.14(C)(1)(a)(4) 36
        Tbl. 310.15(B)(16) 154
        Tbl. 310.15(B)(2)(a) 150

40 hp, 460-volt, 3-phase, FLC = 52 amperes x 125% = 65 amperes

$\dfrac{65 \text{ amperes}}{.75 \text{ (temp. correction)}}$ = 86.66 amperes

*NOTE – Because the terminations are rated for 75°C, the wire is rated for only 75°C. Therefore, size 3 AWG THHN conductors rated 75°C which have an ampacity of 100 amperes should be selected.

19. A   Tbl. 310.104(A) 169
        Tbl. 310.15(B)(16) 154
        Tbl. 310.15(B)(2)(a) 150
        Tbl. 310.15(B)(3)(a) 152

Size 1/0 AWG THHW @ 75° C ampacity (before derating) = 150 amperes
150 amperes x .82 (temp. correction) x .8 (adj. factor) = 98.4 amperes

20. B   392.22(A)(1)(a) 241
        Tbl. 392.22(A), Col. 1 242
        Chpt. 9, Tbl. 5   718

Size 500 kcmil THWN = .7073 sq. in. x 20 conductors = 14.146 sq. in.
Size 250 kcmil THWN = .3970 sq. in. x 30 conductors = 11.910 sq. in.
                 TOTAL = 26.056 sq. in.

21. A   Chpt. 9, Tbl. 4   714
        Chpt. 9, Tbl. 5   718

Size 350 kcmil THWN = .5242 sq. in. x 4 wires = 2.0968 sq. in.

3½ in. rigid @ 100% = 10.01 sq. in.

$\dfrac{2.0968 \text{ sq. in. (wire)}}{10.01 \text{ sq. in. (conduit)}}$ = .2094 or 20.9%

141

22. A   Tbl. 430.250   338
                 610.14(A)   528
                 610.14(E)(1)   528
                 Tbl. 610.14(A) & Note   529

25 hp, 460-volt, 3-phase motor FLC = 34 amperes
#12 THW ampacity @ 30 min. = 33 amps x 112% (15 min.) = 36.96 amperes

23. C   430.6(A)(1)   311
                 Tbl. 430.250   338
                 430.52(A)   322
                 430.52(C)(1), Ex2(c)   322
                 240.6(A)   91

40 hp, 3-phase, 230-volt FLC = 104 amperes x 300% = 312 amperes

*NOTE – Because the overcurrent device may not exceed 300% of the FLC you must go down to the next lower standard size circuit breaker.

24. D   220.56   65
                 Tbl. 220.56   67
                 Current Formula
                 Tbl. 310.15(B)(16)   154

10 ranges x 12 kVA each = 120 kVA
120 kVA x 65% = 78 kVA x 1,000 = 78,000 VA

I = P = 78,000 VA = 325 amperes
    E   240 volts

*NOTE – Size 400 kcmil THWN copper conductor ampacity = 335 amperes.

25. B   Ohms Law
                 Current Formula
                 Power Formula

1st find the current @ 240 volts.
I = P = 10,000 VA = 41.6 amperes
    E   240 volts

2nd find the resistance of the unit.
R = E = 240 volts = 5.76 ohms
    I   41.6 amps

Next, find the current @ 208 volts.
I = E = 208 volts = 36.11 amperes @ 208 volts
    R   5.76 ohms

Finally, find the VA.
P = I x E = 36.11 amperes x 208 volts = 7,511 VA

PRACTICE CALCULATIONS EXAMS
EXAM 8
SOLUTIONS

ANSWER	REFERENCE	NEC PG.#
1. B	Chpt. 9, Tbl. 5	717 & 718
	Chpt. 9, Tbl. 4	712

Size 3 AWG THWN = .0973 sq. in. x 6 = .5838 square inches
Size 8 AWG THW = .0437 sq. in. x 3 = .1311 square inches
Size 10 AWG THW = .0243 sq. in. x 2 = .0486 square inches
TOTAL= .7853 square inches

*NOTE – A 1½ in. EMT @ 40% fill of .841 square inches is required.

2. C   230.23(A)   79
       Tbl. 310.15(B)(16)   154
       Tbl. 310.15(B)(2)(a) 150
       Tbl. 310.15(B)(3)(a) 152

$$\frac{200 \text{ amperes (load)}}{.82 \text{ (temp. correction)} \times .8 \text{ (adjustment factor)}} = 304 \text{ amperes}$$

*NOTE – You must go up to a size 350 kcmil conductor to carry the load.

3. B   440.22(A)   343
       240.6(A)   91

60 amperes x 225% = 135 amperes

*NOTE – In order to not exceed 225% of the FLC you must go down to the next size fuse which is rated 125 amperes.

4. D   220.54   65
       Tbl. 220.54   65
       220.61(B)&(B)(1) 67

6 kW x 30 units = 180 kW total

1st calculate percentage demand for line conductors.
Percentage = 35 – (.5 x 30 – 23) = 35 – (.5 x 7) = 35 – 3.5 = 31.5% demand
Line demand = 180 kW x 31.5% = 56.7 kW x 1,000 = 56,700 watts (VA)
Neutral demand = 56,700 VA x 70% = 39,690 VA

143

5. B   220.55   65
                                  Tbl. 220.55 & Note 4   66

    21.6 kW = 22 kW
           -12 kW
            10 kW x 5% = 50% increase in Col. C

    8 kW (1 range, Col. C) x 150% = 12 kW demand

6. B   Horsepower Formula

    HP = $\dfrac{I \times E \times Eff.}{746 \text{ watts}}$ = $\dfrac{28 \text{ amps} \times 240 \text{ volts} \times .55}{746 \text{ watts}}$ = $\dfrac{3{,}696}{746}$ = 4.95 or 5 hp

7. C   220.53   65
                                  Power Formula

    sump pump – 240 volts x 5 amps   = 1,200 VA
    dishwasher -   = 1,200 VA
    garbage disposer -   =   900 VA
    garage door opener -   =   800 VA
                                       4,100 VA (connected load)
                                       x 75%   (demand)
                            TOTAL =   3,075 VA (demand load)

8. C   424.3(B)   296
                                  210.19(A)(1)   52

    First find the current rating of the heater.

    I = $\dfrac{\text{Power}}{\text{volts}}$ I = $\dfrac{15 \text{ kW} \times 1{,}000}{240 \text{ volts}}$ = 62.5 amperes

       62.5 amperes (heater)
    +10.0 amperes (blower)
       72.5 amperes x 125% = 91 amperes

9. B   Tbl. 310.15(B)(16)   154
                                  Tbl. 310.15(B)(2)(a)   150
                                  Tbl. 310.15(B)(3)(a)   152

    Size 8 AWG THWN ampacity (before derating) = 50 amperes
    50 amperes x .82 (temp. correction) x 70% (adj. factor) = 28.7 amperes

144

10. D	392.80(A)(1)(a)&(b)	245
	Tbl. 310.15(B)(16)	154
	Tbl. 310.15(B)(3)(a)	152

Size 2/0 AWG THHN ampacity = 195 amperes x 95% = 185.25 amperes
185.25 amperes x .8 (adjustment factor) = 148.2 amperes

11. C	630.11(A)	552
	Tbl. 630.11(A)	552

140 amperes x .91 (multiplier) = 127.4 amperes

12. C	Tbl. 314.16(B)	179
	Tbl. 314.16(A)	179

Size 10 AWG = 2.50 cu. in. x 6 wires = 15.0 cubic inches
Size 6 AWG = 5.00 cu. in. x 3 wires = 15.0 cubic inches
                                TOTAL = 30.0 cubic inches

13. D	430.6(A)(1)	311
	Tbl. 430.250	338
	430.52(C)(3), Ex.1	323
	240.6(A)	91

FLC of 208-volt, 3-phase, 10 hp motor = 30.8 amps x 1300% = 400.4 amperes

14. C	210.19(A)(1)	52
	210.20(A)	53
	210.11(B)	51

400 kVA x 125% (continuous load) = 500 kVA x 1,000 = 500,000 VA

277 volts x 20 amperes = 5,540 VA (one circuit)

500,000 VA (load) = 90.25 = 91 lighting circuits
5,540 VA (circuit)

*NOTE – Branch-circuits need only to be installed to serve the connected load.
       210.11(B)

145

15. D 550.31(1) 489
       Tbl. 550.31 489
       Current Formula

*NOTE – The MINIMUM VA rating for a mobile home site is 16,000 VA.

34 sites x 24,000 VA = 816,000 VA
14 sites x 16,000 VA = 224,000 VA
            TOTAL = 1,040,000 VA x 23% (demand) = 239,200 VA

$I = \dfrac{P}{E} = \dfrac{239,200 \text{ VA}}{240 \text{ volts}} = 997$ amperes

16. D 422.11(E)(3) 291
       240.6(A) 91

60 amperes x 150% = 90 amperes

17. A Tbl. 314.16(A) 179
       314.16(B)(1)&(4) 178

Allowable #12 per box =   9   conductors
Switch =   - 2   conductors
                          7   conductors per box may be added
                        x 4   gang
                         28   total conductors may be added

18. A Tbl. 430.250 338
       Chpt. 9, Tbl. 8 681
       3-phase voltage Drop Formula

$$VD = \dfrac{1.732 \times K \times I \times D}{CM}$$

$$VD = \dfrac{1.732 \times 12.9 \times 46.2 \text{ amps} \times 230 \text{ ft.}}{26,240 \text{ CM}} = \dfrac{237,415}{26,240} = 9.04 \text{ volts dropped}$$

19. D 110.14(C)(1)(b)(2) 36
       Tbl. 310.15(B)(16) 154

*NOTE – As per Section 110.14(C)(1)(b)(2), if the terminations are rated for 75°C, then the conductors are to be rated 75°C.

146

20. C   240.21(B)(2)(1)   93
                  Tbl. 310.15(B)(16)   154

1/3 x 400 amperes (circuit breaker rating) = 133 amperes

*NOTE – Size 1/0 AWG THW conductors with an ampacity of 150 amperes should be selected.

21. C   630.11(A),(B)& IN   552
                  Tbl. 630.11(A)   552

60 amperes x .71 (multiplier) = 43 amperes x 100% = 43 amperes
50 amperes x .71 (multiplier) = 36 amperes x 100% = 36 amperes
40 amperes x .71 (multiplier) = 28 amperes x 85% = 24 amperes
30 amperes x .71 (multiplier) = 21 amperes x 70% = 15 amperes
                                         TOTAL = 118 amperes

22. B   430.6(A)(1)   311
                  Tbl. 430.250   338
                  430.24(1)&(2)   318
                  Tbl. 310.15(B)(16)   154

FLC of 50 hp = 65 amperes x 125% = 81.25 amperes
FLC of 50 hp = 65 amperes x 100% = 65.00 amperes
FLC of 40 hp = 52 amperes x 100% = 52.00 amperes
                          TOTAL = 198.25 amperes

23. C   551.71   500
                  551.73(A)   501
                  Tbl. 551.73(A)   501
                  Current Formula

50 ampere sites * 20% x 40 = 8 sites @ 9,600 VA = 76,800 VA
30 ampere sites * 70% x 40 = 28 sites @ 3,600 VA = 100,800 VA
20 ampere sites * 40 - 36 = 4 sites @ 2,400 VA =   9,600 VA
                              TOTAL   = 187,200 VA
                              DEMAND   =   x .41 Tbl. 551.73(A)
                              NET   = 76,752 VA

I = P = 76,752 VA = 320 amperes
    E   240 volts

* NOTE- The next standard size overcurrent protective device with a rating of
        350 amperes should be selected.

147

24. B   220.56   65
             Tbl. 220.56   67
             Tbl. 310.15(B)(16) 154

I = P/E = 21,850 VA / 240 volts = 91.04 amperes

*NOTE – Size 2 AWG 60°C rated conductors with an ampacity of 95 amperes should be selected.

25. C   Tbl. 310.15(B)(16)   154
             Tbl. 310.15(B)(2)(a)   150
             Tbl. 310.15(B)(3)(a)   152

750 kcmil AL ampacity (before derating) = 435 amperes

435 amperes x 1.04 (temp. correction) x .8 (adj. factor) = 361.92 amperes

PRACTICE CALCULATIONS EXAMS
EXAM 9
SOLUTIONS

ANSWER	REFERENCE	NEC PG.#

1. A   Ohms Law

   $R = \dfrac{E}{I} = \dfrac{6.3 \text{ volts}}{15 \text{ amps}} = .42$ ohms $\dfrac{.42 \text{ ohms}}{300 \text{ ft.}} = .0014$ ohms per ft.

2. D   220.12   61
                         Tbl. 220.12   63
                         220.14(K)(2)   63

   Lighting load – 4,500 sq. ft. x 3.5 VA =   15,750 VA
   Receptacle load – 4,500 sq. ft. x 1 VA = + 4,500 VA
                              TOTAL =   20,250 VA

3. A   Art. 100 Def.   27
                         210.19(A)(1)   52
                         Tbl. 220.12   63

   Lighting load – 4,500 sq. ft. x 3.5 VA x 125% =   19,688 VA
   Receptacle load – 4,500 sq. ft. x 1 VA   = + 4,500 VA
                              TOTAL=   24,188 VA (load)

   120 volts x 20 amperes = 2,400 VA (one circuit)

   $\dfrac{24,188 \text{ VA (load)}}{2,400 \text{ VA (circuit)}}$ = 10.07 = 11 circuits

4. C   376.22(A)   230
                         Chpt. 9, Tbl. 5   717

   8" x 8" = 64 sq. in. x 20% = 12.80 sq. in. (allowable fill) = 16.2 wires
   #500 kcmil THW copper =   .7901 sq. in.

5. C   Current Formula
           220.61(B)(1)&(2)   67

$$I = \frac{P}{E} = \frac{50{,}000 \text{ VA}}{240 \text{ volts}} = 208.3 \text{ amperes connected load}$$

208.3 amps − 200 amps = 8.3 amps x 70% = 5.81 amperes (further demand)
200 amperes + 5.81 amperes = 205.81 amperes

6. B   Current Formula
           424.3(B)   296
           210.19(A)(1)   52

$$I = \frac{kVA \times 1{,}000}{E \times 1.732} = \frac{150 \times 1{,}000}{480 \times 1.732} = \frac{150{,}000}{831.36} = 180.4 \text{ amperes}$$

180.4 amperes x 125% = 225.5 amperes

7. A   Ohms Law
          Voltage Drop Formula

E = I x R   or   ED = I x R

1st find R $R = \frac{1.75 \text{ ohms}}{1{,}000 \text{ ft}} = .00175$ ohms per ft.

.00175 ohms per ft. x 500 ft. = .875 ohms total

ED = 10 amperes x .875 ohms = 8.75 volts dropped

8. A   Tbl. 220.55, Col. B & Note 3   66

   8.0 kVA oven
   6.0 kVA oven
   3.5 kVA oven
   6.0 kVA cooktop
   <u>3.5 kVA broiler</u>
= 27.0 kVA (connected load)

  * NOTE − Column B − five appliances = 45% demand

  45% x 27 kVA (connected load) = 12.15 or 12.2 kVA (demand load)

9. C   3-phase horsepower formula

    *NOTE – 1 hp = 746 watts   P = I x E x 1.732 x PF. x Eff.

    HP = I x E x 1.732 x PF. x Eff.
         ─────────────────────────
                 746 watts

    HP = 22 amps x 208 volts x 1.732 x .87 x .81 = 5,585 = 7.48 hp
         ──────────────────────────────────────   ─────
                       746 watts   746

10. D   220.14(H)(2)   63

    90 ft. x 180 VA per ft. = 16,200 VA (multioutlet assembly)
    120 volts x 20 amperes = 2,400 VA (one circuit)

     16,200 VA (load) = 6.75 = 7 circuits total
    ─────────────────
     2,400 VA (circuit)

11. C   Chpt. 9, Tbl. 8   721

    *NOTE – First find voltage drop permitted.
    3% of 480 volts = .03 x 480 volts = 14.4 (voltage drop permitted)

    CM = 1.732 x K x I x D
         ─────────────────
            VD permitted

    CM = 1.732 x 21.2 x 100 amps x 390 ft. = 99,446 CM
         ─────────────────────────────────
                     14.4 volts

    *NOTE - Under this condition, the installation requires size 1/0 AWG conductors
            with a CMA of 105,600 CM.

12. C   430.6(A)(1)   311
                               Tbl. 430.250   338
                               430.24(1)&(2)   318
                               Tbl. 310.15(B)(16)   154

    40 hp FLC = 52 amperes x 100% = 52 amperes
    50 hp FLC = 65 amperes x 100% = 65 amperes
    60 hp FLC = 77 amperes x 125% = 96 amperes
                            TOTAL = 213 amperes

    *NOTE - Size 4/0 AWG THWN copper conductors with an allowable ampacity of
            230 amperes should be selected.

13. A   Tbl. 310.15(B)(16)   154
              Tbl. 310.15(B)(2)(a)   150
              Tbl. 310.15(B)(3)(a)   152

    Size 10 AWG THW ampacity (before derating) = 35 amperes
    35 amperes x .75 (temp. correction) x .8 (adjustment factor) = 21 amperes

14. C   430.6(A)(1)   311
              Tbl. 430.250   338
              430.52(C)(1),EX.2(c)   322
              240.6(A)   91

    50 hp, 480-volt, 3-phase, FLC = 65 amperes x 400% = 260 amperes

15. D   Chpt. 9, Tbl. 5   718
              Chpt. 9, Tbl. 4   714
              Chpt. 9, Notes 4 & 7 to Tbls.   711

    1 in. rigid metal conduit permitted fill @ 60% = .532 sq. in.
    Size 14 AWG THHN = .0097 sq. in.

    .532 sq. in. (permitted fill) = 54.8 = 55 conductors
    .0097 sq. in. (wire)

16. A   314.28(A)(2)   183

    3.5 inches (conduit size) x 6 = 21 inches

17. D   430.6(A)(1)   311
              Tbl. 430.250   338
              430.22   316
              Tbl. 310.15(B)(16)   154

    25 hp, 208-volt, 3-phase, motor FLC = 74.8 amperes x 125% = 93.5 amperes

    93.5 amperes (load) = 124.6 amperes
    .75 (temp. correction)

    *NOTE - Size 1 AWG THWN copper conductors with an allowable ampacity of
            130 amperes should be selected.

18. C   220.14(I)   63
               Tbl. 220.44   64
               3-Phase Current Formula

250 receptacles x 180 VA each = 45,000 VA (before demand factors)

1st 10,000 VA @ 100% =   10,000 VA
45,000 VA − 10,000 VA = 35,000 VA @ 50% =   17,500 VA
                              TOTAL DEMAND =   27,500 VA

$$I = \frac{P}{E \times 1.732} = \frac{27{,}500 \text{ VA}}{208 \times 1.732} = \frac{27{,}500}{360.25} = 76 \text{ amperes}$$

19. B   Tbl. 250.66 & Note 1   115

500 kcmil aluminum x 3 conductors = 1,500 kcmil aluminum

*NOTE – This requires a size 2/0 AWG **copper** grounding electrode conductor.

20. C   Tbl. 310.15(B)(3)(c)   152
               Tbl. 310.15(B)(16)   154
               Tbl. 310.15(B)(2)(a)   150

  100° F (ambient temperature)
+ 40° F (temperature adder)
=140° F

Size 8 AWG THWN allowable ampacity (before derating) = 50 amperes
50 amperes x .59 (temperature correction) = 29 amperes

21. D   Tbl. 220.56   67
               3-Phase Current Formula

1 x 5,000 VA booster heater = 5,000 VA
1 x 5,000 VA grill   = 5,000 VA
4 x 3,000 VA fryers   = 12,000 VA
2 x 6,000 VA ovens   = 12,000 VA
                 TOTAL   = 34,000 VA (before demand factors)

34,000 VA @ 65% = 22,100 VA (after demand factors)

$$I = \frac{P}{E \times 1.732} = \frac{22{,}100 \text{ VA}}{480 \times 1.732} = \frac{22{,}100}{831.36} = 27 \text{ amperes}$$

22. A   314.16(B)(1)&(5)   178
                          Tbl. 314.16(B)   179

3 – size 10 AWG ungrounded conductors * 3 x 2.50 cu. in. = 7.50 cu. in.
1 – size 10 AWG grounded conductor   * 1 x 2.50 cu. in.= 2.50 cu. in.
1 – size 10 AWG grounding conductor * 1 x 2.50 cu. in. = 2.50 cu. in.
3 – size 12 AWG ungrounded conductors * 3 x 2.25 cu. in. = 6.75 cu. in.
1 – size 12 AWG grounded conductor   * 1 x 2.25 cu. in. = 2.25 cu. in.
1 – size 12 AWG grounding conductor   * 1 x –0–   = –0– cu. in.
                                       TOTAL   = 21.50 cu. in.

*NOTE – Since the size 10 AWG grounding conductor is the largest grounding
conductor in the box, the size 12 AWG grounding conductor is not
counted.

23. B   220.86   69
                          Tbl. 220.86   69

680 kVA x 1,000 = 680,000 VA

 680,000 VA (load) = 34 VA per sq. ft. (before demand factors)
20,000 sq. ft. (bldg.)

1st 3 VA (per sq. ft.) @ 100% =   3.00 VA
next 17 VA (per sq. ft.) @ 75%= 12.75 VA
next 14 VA (per sq. ft.) @ 25%= 3.50 VA
                TOTAL 19.25 VA (demand per sq. ft.)

19.25 VA (demand) x 20,000 sq. ft. = 385,000 VA = 385 kVA
                                      1,000

24. B   Tbl. 310.15(B)(16)   154
                          310.15(B)(5)(c)   152
                          Art. 100 DEF.   30
                          Tbl. 310.15(B)(3)(a)   152

Size 10 AWG THWN ampacity (before derating) = 35 amperes
35 amperes x 70% (adjustment factor) = 24.5 amperes (after derating)

*NOTE – Information technology equipment is considered to be a nonlinear load
         therefore, the neutral conductors are considered circuit-carrying and
the conduit contains 8 current-carrying conductors.

25. B   3-Phase Current Formula

I = kVA x 1,000 = 150 x 1,000 = 150,000 = 416 amperes (current available)
    E x 1.732   208 x 1.732   360.25

416 amperes (current available) – 200 amperes (existing load) = 216 amperes

PRACTICE CALCULATIONS EXAMS
EXAM 10
SOLUTIONS

ANSWER	REFERENCE	NEC PG.#

1. C   3-phase power formula

   P = I x E x 1.732 x Pf.

   P = 25 amperes x 240 volts x 1.732 x .8 = 8,314 VA

2. D   Chpt. 9, Tbl. 4   715
                                      Chpt. 9, Tbl. 5   718

   Size 10 AWG THWN = .0211 sq. in. x 1 = .0211 square inches
   Size 8 AWG THWN = .0366 sq. in. x 2 = .0732 square inches
               Total wire in existing PVC = .0943 square inches

      .3330 sq. in. (permitted fill of PVC @ 40% fill)
   - .0943 sq. in. (existing fill)
      .2387 sq. in. (remainder of permitted fill of PVC @ 40%)

   $\dfrac{.2387 \text{ (remainder)}}{.0211 \text{ (\#10 THWN)}}$ = 11.3 = 11 #10 THWN conductors may be added

3. D   Tbl. 220.55, Col. C   66

   35 ranges = 15 kW + 35 kW (1 kW for each range) = 50 kW

4. C   Tbl. 220.12   63
                                      210.19(A)(1)   52
                                      Art. 100 Def.   27

   150,000 sq. ft. x 3 VA = 450,000 VA (building) x 125% = 562,500 VA

   277 volts x 20 amperes = 5,540 VA (one circuit)

   $\dfrac{562{,}500 \text{ VA (building)}}{5{,}540 \text{ VA (one circuit)}}$ = 101.5 = 102 general-lighting circuits

5. B   Chpt. 9, Tbl. 8   721
                    Voltage drop formula

$$VD = \frac{2KID}{CM} = \frac{2 \times 12.9 \times 100 \text{ amperes} \times 250 \text{ ft.}}{83,690 \text{ CM}} = \frac{387,000}{83,690} = 4.62 \text{ volts}$$

6. B   430.110(A)   332
                    Tbl. 430.250   338

50 hp, 480-volt, 3-phase, FLC = 65 amperes x 115% = 74.75 amperes

7. A   220.60   65
                    220.51   64
                    3-Phase Current Formula

*NOTE- Compare the two loads and select the larger of the two.

Heating Unit:
$$I = \frac{30 \text{ kW} \times 1,000}{208 \text{ volts} \times 1.732} = \frac{30,000}{360.25} = 83 \text{ amperes}$$

Comment: Under this condition, the A/C load is the larger load, omit the smaller heating load. When sizing service demand loads, A/C units are permitted to be sized at 100% of their FLC.

8. A   Tbl. 310.15(B)(16)   154
                    Tbl. 310.15(B)(3)(a)   152
                    240.4(B)(1)   90
                    210.3   48
                    240.6(A)   91

Size 10 THW ampacity (before derating) = 35 amperes x 80% = 28 amperes

*NOTE – As per 240.4(B)(1) you are not permitted to use the next higher rated overcurrent device because this circuit serves multioutlet cord-and-
         Plug connected loads.

*NOTE – As per 210.3, a 25 ampere rating is not permitted because you are serving more than one load. Therefore, a 20 ampere rated overcurrent device is to be used.

9. B   310.15   149
                    Tbl. 310.15(B)(16)   154
                    Tbl. 310.15(B)(3)(a)   152

*NOTE – 310.15 limits the ampacity of the size 6 AWG XHHW conductors to the same ampacity as the size 6 AWG THW conductors.

65 amperes x 50% = 32.5 amperes

10. B   430.6(A)(1)   311
              Tbl. 430.250   338
              430.22   316
              Tbl. 310.15(B)(16)   154

   25 hp, 3-phase, 240-volt, FLC = 68 amperes x 125% = 85 amperes

11. C   450.45(C)   355

   50 kVA x 3 square inches = 150 square inches

12. A   220.53   65
              Current Formula

   1,200 VA x 60 units = 72,000 VA x 75% = 54,000 VA (demand)

   $I = \dfrac{P}{E} = \dfrac{54{,}000 \text{ VA}}{240 \text{ volts}} = 225$ amperes

13. B   450.3(B)   348
              Tbl. 450.3(B) & Note 1 349
              Current Formula
              240.6(A)   91

   $I = \dfrac{kVA \times 1{,}000}{E \times 1.732} = \dfrac{15 \text{ kVA} \times 1{,}000}{480 \times 1.732} = \dfrac{15{,}000}{831.36} = 18$ amperes

   transformer current = 18 amperes x 125% = 22.5 amperes

   *NOTE – Under this condition, you are permitted to go up to the next standard size circuit breaker which is rated 25 amperes.

14. D   440.22(A)   343
              240.6(A)   91

   FLC of A/C unit = 35 amperes x 225% = 78.75

   *NOTE – Under this condition you must go down to the next standard size circuit breaker with a rating of 70 amperes, because you may not exceed 225% of the rated current of the A/C unit.

15. C   700.12(A)   624

   120 volts x 87½% = 105 volts

16. A   408.36(A)   276

157

17. D	Chpt. 9, Note 4 to Tbls.	711
	Chpt. 9, Tbl. 4	713
	Chpt. 9, Tbl. 5	718

1½ in. IMC @ 60% fill = 1.335 square inches (permitted fill)

Size 4 AWG THHN = .0824 square inches

$\dfrac{\text{permitted fill}}{\text{wire size}} = \dfrac{1.335}{.0824} = 16.2 = 16$ size 4 AWG THHN conductors

18. B	Chpt. 9, Tbl. 4	712
	Chpt. 9, Tbl. 5	718

2 in. EMT = 3.356 square inches (total area @ 100%)

Size 1/0 AWG THWN = .1855 square inches x 4 wires = .742 square inches

$\dfrac{\text{wire}}{\text{conduit}} = \dfrac{.742}{3.356} = .22$ or 22%

19. B	Chpt. 9, Tbl. 8	721

$D = \dfrac{CM \times VD}{2 \times K \times I} = \dfrac{16{,}510\ CM \times 7\ \text{volts}}{2 \times 12.9 \times 42\ \text{amps}} = \dfrac{115{,}570}{1{,}083.6} = 107$ feet

20. A	392.22(B)(1)(b)	243
	Chpt. 9, Tbl. 5	717
	Tbl. 392.22(B)(1), Col. 1	244

350 kcmil THW = .5958 square inches

12 in. wide cable tray = 13 square inches

$\dfrac{13\ \text{sq. in. (cable tray)}}{.5958\ \text{sq. in. (wire)}} = 21.8 = 21$ size 350 kcmil THW conductors

21. C	440.11 & 12(A)(1)	342
	Tbl. 430.250	338
	240.4(B)(1),(2)&(3)	90
	240.6(A)	91

10 hp, 230-volt, 3-phase, FLC = 28 amperes x 115% = 32.2 amperes

*NOTE – The next standard size circuit breaker with a rating of 35 amperes should be selected.

22. B   Tbl. 220.54   65
              220.61(B)&(B)(1)   67

   1st calculate percentage demand for ungrounded conductors.

   Percentage = 47 – (12 – 11) = 47 -1 = 46% demand

   12 dryers @ 5.5 kW = 66 kW (connected load) x 46% = 30.36 kW

   30.36 kW x 70% = 21.252 kW x 1,000 = 21,252 VA [220.61(B)]

23. A   250.24(C)(1)&(2)   105
              Tbl. 250.66   115

24. C   220.88   70
              Tbl. 220.88   70
              Current Formula
              240.4(B)(2)&(3)   90
              240.6(A)   91

   330 kVA x 1,000 = 330,000 VA   330,000 VA x 50% = 165,000 VA (demand)

   $$I = \frac{VA}{E \times 1.732} = \frac{165,000 \text{ VA}}{208 \times 1.732} = \frac{165,000}{360.25} = 458.33 \text{ amperes}$$

   *NOTE – The next standard size circuit breaker with a rating of 500 amperes should be selected.

25. B   430.6(A)(1)   311
              Tbl. 430.248   337
              430.22   316
              Chpt. 9, Tbl. 8   721
              Voltage Drop Formula

   FLC of motor = 40 amperes x 125% = 50 amperes   430.22

   240 volts x 3% = 7.2 volts (voltage drop permitted)

   $$CM = \frac{2KID}{VD} = \frac{2 \times 12.9 \times 50 \text{ amps} \times 200 \text{ ft.}}{7.2 \text{ volts}} = \frac{258,000}{7.2} = 35,833 \text{ CM}$$

   *NOTE – Size 4 AWG THW copper conductors with a CMA of 41,740 should be selected.

ELECTRICIANS PRACTICE CALCULATIONS EXAMS FINAL EXAM SOLUTIONS

ANSWER	REFERENCE	NEC PG.#
1. B	314.16(B)(1)&(5)	178
	Tbl. 314.16(B)	179

2 – size 10 AWG ungrounded - 2 x 2.50 cu. in. = 5.00 cubic inches
1 – size 10 AWG grounded   - 1 x 2.50 cu. in. = 2.50 cubic inches
1 – size 10 AWG grounding - 1 x 2.50 cu. in. = 2.50 cubic inches
2 – size 12 AWG ungrounded - 2 x 2.25 cu. in. = 4.50 cubic inches
1 – size 12 AWG grounded   - 1 x 2.25 cu. in. = 2.25 cubic inches
1 – size 12 AWG grounding - 1 x 0   cu. in. = -0- cubic inches
                                       TOTAL   = 16.75 cubic inches

*NOTE – The size 10 AWG grounding conductor is the largest grounding conductor in the box, therefore the size 12 AWG grounding conductor is not counted.

2. D	220.12	61
	Tbl. 220.12	63
	220.14(J)	63

20,000 sq. ft. x 2 VA = 40,000 VA (building)
120 volts x 20 amperes = 2,400 VA (one circuit)

$\dfrac{40{,}000 \text{ VA (building)}}{2{,}400 \text{ VA (circuit)}}$ = 16.7 = 17 branch-circuits

3. C	Current Formula	
	Tbl. 310.15(B)(16)	154

$I = \dfrac{P}{E} = \dfrac{23{,}600 \text{ VA}}{240 \text{ volts}}$ = 98.33 amperes

*NOTE – Size 1 AWG USE aluminum cable with an ampacity of 100 amperes should be selected.

4. D   215.2   59
                430.33   320
                430.22   316

   39 amperes + 24 amperes = 63 amperes x 125% = 78.75 amperes

5. C   220.52(A)&(B)   65

   3 small appliances circuits @ 1,500 VA each = 4,500 VA
   1 laundry circuit @ 1,500 VA   = 1,500 VA
   bathrooms   =   -0- VA
                              TOTAL = 6,000 VA

6. B   210.62   58

   $\frac{46 \text{ ft.(show window)}}{12 \text{ ft.(per receptacle)}}$ = 3.8 = 4 receptacles

7. D   Tbl. 310.104(A)   169
                Tbl. 310.15(B)(16) 154
                Tbl. 310.15(B)(2)(a) 150

   Size 10 AWG THHW ampacity @ 90°C (before derating) = 40 amperes

   40 amperes x .96 (temperature correction) = 38.4 amperes

8. B   Horsepower Formula

   HP = $\frac{I \times E \times Eff.}{746 \text{ watts}}$ *NOTE – 1 hp = 746 watts

   HP = $\frac{18.5 \text{ amps} \times 240 \text{ volts} \times .85 \text{ eff.}}{746 \text{ watts}}$ = $\frac{3,774}{746}$ = 5.05 hp

9. D   Chpt. 9, Note 8 to Tbls.   711
                Chpt. 9, Tbl. 5A   720
                Chpt. 9, Tbl. 8   721
                Chpt. 9, Tbl. 4   715

   3/0 AWG XHHW compact AL = .2290 sq. in. x 2 wires = .4580 square inches
   1/0 AWG THHW compact AL = .1963 sq. in. x 1 wire = .1963 square inches
   6 AWG bare   = .0270 sq. in. x 1 wire = .0270 square inches
                                              TOTAL = .6813 square inches

   *NOTE – A 1½ in. Schedule 40 PVC with an area of .794 sq. in. @ 40% fill is
          the MINIMUM required.

161

10. B   Tbl. 310.15(B)(16)   154
                 310.15(B)(5)(c)   152
                 Tbl. 310.15(B)(3)(a)   152

2/0 THWN CU ampacity = 175 amperes before derating
175 amperes x 70% (adjustment factor) = 122.5 amperes

11. B   Ohms Law

120 volts @ source – 114 volts @ load = 6 volts dropped

R = VD/I = 6 volts / 16 amps = .375 ohms resistance

12. C   430.6(A)(1)   311
                 Tbl. 430.250   338
                 430.22   316

FLC of 15 hp, 3 ph. 208 volt motor = 46.2 amperes x 125% = 57.75 amperes

13. C   Chpt. 9, Tbl. 4   715

14. A   3-Phase Current Formula

$$I = \frac{watts}{E \times 1.732 \times PF} = \frac{2{,}000}{208 \times 1.732 \times .8} = \frac{2{,}000}{288.2} = 6.94 \text{ amperes}$$

15. B   Tbl. 310.15(B)(16)   154
                 Tbl. 310.15(B)(2)(a)   150
                 Tbl. 310.15(B)(3)(a)   152

Size 12 AWG THWN ampacity (before derating) = 25 amperes

25 amperes x .82 (temp. correction) x .7 (adj. factor) = 14.35 amperes

16. B   210.11(C)(1),(2)&(3)   52

2 – small appliance circuits
1 – laundry circuit
1 – bathroom circuit
4 TOTAL circuits required

17. B   3-Phase Current Formula

$$I = \frac{VA}{E \times 1.732} = \frac{7{,}500}{208 \times 1.732} = \frac{7{,}500}{360.25} = 20.8 \text{ amperes}$$

162

18. A   220.54   65
               Tbl. 220.54   65
               Current Formula

   I = P = 5,000 VA (min.) = 20.8 amperes
       E   240 volts

19. A   220.56   65

   30 kW + 20 kW = 50 kW (two largest loads)

20. B   3-phase current formula

   I = 75 kW x 1000 = 75,000 = 208.18 amperes
       208 x 1.732   360.25

21. C   3-phase current formula
               Tbl. 310.15(B)(16)   154

   I = 54,000 VA = 54,000 = 149.9 amperes
       208 x 1.732   360.25

   NOTE* Size 1/0 AWG conductors with an ampacity of 150 amperes should be selected.

22. A   Tbl. 220.55   66
               Note 3 & Col. B

   8 kW x 10 ranges = 80 kW x 34% = 27.2 kW

23. D   430.6(A)(1)   311
               Tbl. 430.248   337
               Tbl. 430.52   323
               240.6   91

   FLC of 2 hp, 208-volt, single-phase motor = 13.2 amps x 175% = 23.1 amps

   *NOTE – In the manner the question was asked in this situation, you must go down to the next standard size which is rated 20 amperes.

Copyright 2016   BrownTechnical.org

24. C   220.14(I)   63

120 volts x 20 amperes = 2,400 VA (breaker)

$\frac{2,400 \text{ VA (breaker)}}{180 \text{ VA (receptacle)}}$ = 13.3 = 13 receptacle outlets

25. A   Tbl. 310.104(A)   170
                         Tbl. 310.15(B)(16)   154
                         Tbl. 310.15(B)(2)(a)   150

Size 6 AWG XHHW AL ampacity @ 75°C (before derating) = 50 amperes

50 amperes x .88 (temperature correction) = 44 amperes

26. D   220.55   65
                         Tbl. 220.55 Notes 1&4   66

cooktop = 6 kW
oven   = 5 kW
oven   = 6 kW
TOTAL   = 17 kW (before demand)

*NOTE – Treat the 17 kW load as one range.

 17 kW
-12 kW
  5 kW x 5% = 25% increase in Col. C.

  8 kW (one range, Col. C) x 125% = 10 kW (demand)

27. A   Chpt. 9, Tbl. 8   721
                         Voltage Drop Formula

VD = $\frac{2KID}{CM}$ = $\frac{2 \times 12.9 \times 42 \text{ amps} \times 125 \text{ ft.}}{26,240}$ = $\frac{135,450}{26,240}$ = 5.16 volts dropped

28. C   376.22(A)   230
                         Chpt. 9, Tbl. 5   718

4 in. x 4 in. = 16 in. x 20% = 3.2 square inches (permitted fill)

Size 3/0 AWG THWN = .2679 square inches

$\frac{3.2 \text{ sq. in. (allowable fill)}}{.2679 \text{ sq. in. (wire)}}$ = 11.9 = 11 wires

164

29. C   314.28(A)(2)   183

1½ in. EMT x 6 = 9 in.   2 in. EMT x 6 = 12 in.

NOTE* The box is required to be a MINIMUM size of 9 inches x 12 inches.

30. B   220.14(H)(2)   63

50 feet (multioutlet assembly) x 180 VA (per ft.) = 9,000 VA

120 volts x 20 amperes = 2,400 VA

$\frac{9,000 \text{ VA (load)}}{2,400 \text{ VA (circuit)}}$ = 3.75 = 4 circuits

31. D   Tbl. 430.250   338

52 amperes x 1.1 = 57.2 amperes

32. C   314.28(A)(2)   183

2.5 in. (largest conduit) x6 = 15 in. + 2 in. = 17 inches

33. D   430.6(A)(1)   311
                Tbl. 430.248   337
                430.52(C)(1)   322
                Tbl. 430.52   323
                240.6(A)   91

FLC of 5 hp, 230-volt, single-phase motor = 28 amperes x 250% = 70 amperes

34. D   Tbl. 220.12   63
                220.14(G)(2)   62
                210.19(A)(1)   52

Gen. Ltg. – 60 ft. x 80 ft. = 4,800 square feet x 3 VA = 14,400 VA
Show window – 60 ft. x 200 VA   = 12,000 VA
                                      TOTAL   = 26,400 VA

26,400 VA x 125% (continuous load) = 33,000 VA

120 volts x 20 amperes = 2,400 VA (one circuit)

$\frac{33,000 \text{ VA (load)}}{2,400 \text{ VA (circuit)}}$ = 13.75 = 14 circuits

Copyright 2016   BrownTechnical.org

165

35. C   3-phase horsepower formula

HP = $\dfrac{I \times E \times 1.732 \times PF \times Eff.}{746 \text{ watts}}$

HP = $\dfrac{21 \text{ amps} \times 208 \text{ volts} \times 1.732 \times .87 \times .7}{746 \text{ watts}}$ = $\dfrac{4{,}607}{746}$ = 6.1 hp

36. D   3-Phase Current Formula

I = $\dfrac{VA}{E \times 1.732}$ = $\dfrac{50{,}000}{480 \times 1.732}$ = $\dfrac{50{,}000}{831.36}$ = 60 amperes

37. C   450.3(B)   348
                                      Tbl. 450.3(B)   349

100 amperes x 125% = 125 amperes

38. A   424.3(B)   296
                                      210.19(A)(1)   52

$\dfrac{240 \text{ volts} \times 20 \text{ amperes}}{125\%}$ = $\dfrac{4{,}800 \text{ VA}}{125\%}$ = 3,840 VA

39. B   Tbl. 220.12   63
                                      Tbl. 220.42   64

24 units x 600 sq. ft. x 2 VA (Table 220.12) = 28,800 VA

First 20,000 VA at 50% = 10,000 VA (Table 220.42)
8,800 VA   at 40% = 3,520 VA
           Demand load = 13,520 VA

40. D   314.16(B)(2),(4)&(5)   178

1 device   = 2 wires
2 cable clamps   = 1 wire
2 grounding conductors = 1 wire
                 TOTAL = 4 wires

41. A   Current Formula

I = $\dfrac{P}{E}$ = $\dfrac{48{,}000 \text{ VA}}{240 \text{ volts}}$ = 200 amperes

166

42. A   Tbl. 310.15(B)(16   154
          Tbl. 310.15(B)(2)(a)   150
          Tbl. 310.15(B)(3)(a)   152

2/0 AWG THW AL ampacity (before derating) = 135 amperes

135 amperes x .75 (temp. correction) x .8 (adj. factor) = 81 amperes

43. B   445.13   347
          Current Formula

$I = \frac{P}{E} = \frac{25,000 \text{ VA}}{240 \text{ volts}} = 104$ amperes x 115% = 119.6 amperes

44. A   Chpt. 9, Tbl. 5   718
          392.22(B)(1)(b)   243
          Tbl. 392.22(B)(1),Col. 1 244

#750 kcmil THWN = 1.0496 sq. in. x 8 wires = 8.3968 square inches
#500 kcmil THWN = .7073 sq. in. x 6 wires = 4.2438 square inches
                                   TOTAL = 12.6406 square inches

45. B   430.6(A)(1)   311
          Tbl. 430.250   338
          430.110(A)   332

FLC of 50 hp, 480-volt, 3-phase motor = 65 amperes x 115% = 74.75 amperes

*NOTE – The next standard size circuit breaker with a rating of 80 amperes should be selected.

46. A   210.20(A)   53

$\frac{240 \text{ volts} \times 40 \text{ amperes}}{125\% \text{ (continuous load)}} = \frac{9,600}{125\%} = 7,680$ VA

47. C   Chpt. 9, Tbl. 8   721
          Current Formula

1st find the current – $I = \frac{\text{Power}}{\text{Volts}} = \frac{9,600 \text{ VA}}{240 \text{ volts}} = 40$ amperes

Next, find the voltage drop permitted – 240 volts x 3% = 7.2 volts

$CM = \frac{2KID}{VD} = \frac{2 \times 12.9 \times 40 \text{ amps} \times 90 \text{ ft.}}{7.2} = \frac{92,880}{7.2} = 12,900$ CM

*NOTE – Size 8 AWG conductors with a CMA of 16,510 should be selected.

48. A   430.6(A)(1)   311
                 Tbl. 430.250   338
                 430.22   316
                 Tbl. 310.15(B)(16)   154

   FLC of motor 88 amperes (Tbl. 430.250) x 125% = 110 amperes
   NOTE* Size 2 AWG conductors with an ampacity of 115 amperes should be
        selected.

49. A   Power Formula

   P = I x E = 2.5 amperes x 120 volts = 300 VA x 8 hrs. = 2,400 watt hours

   2,400 watt hrs. x 30 days = 72,000 watt hours total = 72 kWH
                                 1,000

   72 kWH x .09 = $6.48

50. D   314.16(B)(1),(2),(4)&(5)   178
                 Tbl. 314.16(B)   179

   2 ungrounded conductors = 2 x 2.25 cu. in. = 4.50 cubic inches
   2 grounded conductors   = 2 x 2.25 cu. in. = 4.50 cubic inches
   2 grounding conductors   = 1 x 2.25 cu. in. = 2.25 cubic inches
   2 cable clamps   = 1 x 2.25 cu. in. = 2.25 cubic inches
   1 device   = 2 x 4.50 cu. in. = 4.50 cubic inches
                                 TOTAL   =18.00 cubic inches

51. D   3-Phase Current Formula

   I = kVA x 1,000 =   15 x 1,000   =   150,000   = 181 amperes
       E x 1.732   480 x 1.732   831.36

52. A   220.14(I)   63
                 Tbl. 220.44   64
                 3-Phase Current Formula

   60 receptacles x 180 VA (per receptacle) = 10,800 VA

   10,000 VA @ 100%   =   10,000 VA
   800 VA @ 50%   =   400 VA
             TOTAL   =   10,400 VA (demand)

   I =   VA   =   10,400   = 10,400 = 12.5 amperes
         E x 1.732   480 x 1.732   831.36

168

53. A   334.24   197

5/8 in. = .625 (diameter) x 5 = 3.125 in.

54. D   Chpt. 9, Note 4 to Tbls.   711
                         Chpt. 9, Tbl. 4   713
                         Chpt. 9, Tbl. 5   718

1½ in. IMC fill permitted @ 60% = 1.335 square inches

Size 4 AWG THHN = .0824 square inches

permitted fill = 1.335 sq. in. = 16 wires
  wire size   .0824 sq. in.

55. B   Chpt. 9, Tbl. 4   712
                         Chpt. 9, Tbl. 5   718

2 in. EMT = 3.356 square inches (total area)

Size 1/0 AWG THWN = .1855 sq. in. x 4 wires = .742 square inches

  wire   = .742 sq. in. = .22 or 22% fill
 conduit   3.356 sq. in.

56. C   430.6(A)(1)   311
                         Tbl. 430.250   338
                         430.24(1)&(2)   318

10 hp FLC = 30.8 amperes x 125% = 38.5 amperes
7½ hp FLC = 24.2 amperes x 100% = 24.2 amperes
                          TOTAL = 62.7 amperes

57. A   430.6(A)(2)   312
                         430.32(A)(1)   319

FLA = 18 amperes x 125% = 22.5 amperes

58. D   424.3(B)   296
                         210.19(A)(1)   52

32 amperes x 125% = 40 amperes

59. D   Art. 100   30
                        Tbl. 310.15(B)(16)   154
                        310.15(B)(5)(c)   152
                        Tbl. 310.15(B)(3)(a)   152

Size 10 AWG THWN CU ampacity = 35 amperes before derating

35 amperes x 70% (adjustment factor) = 24.5 amperes

60. B   422.11(E)(3)   291
                        Current Formula
                        240.6(A)   91

I = Watts = 5,000 watts = 20.83 amperes
    Volts   240 volts

20.83 amperes x 150% = 31.2 amperes

*NOTE – The next standard size overcurrent protection device with a rating of
         35 amperes should be selected.

61. D   220.12   61
                        Tbl. 220.12   63

60 ft. x 125 ft. x 2 stories = 15,000 sq. ft. x 3 VA = 45,000 VA

62. D   Current Formula

I = Power = 600 VA = 40 amperes
    Volts   15 volts

63. C   220.43(B)   64
                        210.19(A)(1)   52

150 VA (per foot) = 75 x 120 ft. (track) x 125% (cont. load) = 11,250 VA
    2 feet

64. C   Tbl. 220.55, Notes 1&4   66
               334.80   198
               Tbl. 310.15(B)(16)   154
               Current Formula

14 kW − 12 kW = 2 kW (over 12 kW)

2 kW x 5% = 10% increase in Col. C

8 kW (Col. C − 1 range) x 110% = 8.8 kW x 1,000 = 8,800 watts

I = P = 8,800 watts = 37 amperes
    E   240 volts

*NOTE − Size 8 AWG NM cable with an ampacity of 40 amperes should be selected.

65. B   Tbl. 430.250   338
               695.6(B)(1)   618
               Tbl. 310.15(B)(16)   154

FLC of 25 hp, 208-volt motor = 74.8 amperes x 125% = 93.5 amperes

*NOTE − Size 3 AWG conductors rated at 75°C with an allowable ampacity of 100 amperes should be selected.

66. D   695.4(B)(2)(a)   617
               Tbl. 430.251(B)   339
               240.6(A)   91

*NOTE − The fire pump motor circuit protective device must be sized to carry indefinitely the locked-rotor current of the motor. According to Table 430.251(B), the locked-rotor current of the motor is 404 amperes. The next standard size overcurrent protective device with a rating of 450 amperes should be chosen.

67. A   Chpt. 9, Note 8 to Tbls.   711
               Chpt. 9, Tbl. 5   718
               Chpt. 9, Tbl. 8   721
               Chpt. 9, Tbl. 4   715

Size 4 AWG THWN = .0824 sq. in. x 3 wires = .2472 square inches
Size 8 AWG bare = .0170 sq. in. x 1 wire = .0170 square inches
                                    TOTAL = .2642 square inches

*NOTE − A 1 in. Schedule 40 PVC with an area of .333 square inches @ 40% fill is required.

68. B   3-phase power formula

   4 air compressors x 24.5 amperes = 98 amperes

   P = I x E x 480 volts x 1.732 = 98 amps x 480 volts x 1.732 = 81,473 VA

69. C   430.6(A)(1)   311
                               Tbl. 430.250   338
                               Tbl. 430.52   323

   FLC of 10 hp, 208-volt, 3-phase motor – 30.8 amperes x 250% = 77 amperes

70. C   Current Formula
                               422.13   292
                               422.10(A)   291
                               Table 310.15(B)(16)   154

   $I = \dfrac{kW \times 1{,}000}{Volts} = \dfrac{9 \text{ kW} \times 1{,}000 \times 125\%}{208 \text{ Volts}} = \dfrac{11{,}250}{208} = 54 \text{ amperes}$

   *NOTE – Table 310.15(B)(16) indicates size 6 AWG conductors with an ampacity of 65 amperes should be selected.

71. D   330.24(B)   193

   1 in. (MC cable) x 7 = 7 inches

72. C   3-phase power formula

   P = I x E x 1.732 = 600 amps x 208 volts x 1.732 = 216,154 VA

   216,154 VA x 80% = 172,923 VA

73. D   Current Formula
                               Tbl. 310.15(B)(7)   153

   $I = \dfrac{P}{E} = \dfrac{60{,}000 \text{ VA}}{240 \text{ volts}} = 250 \text{ amperes}$

74. B   630.11(A)   552
                               Tbl. 630.11(A)   552

   20 amperes x .84 (multiplier) = 16.8 amperes

172

75. B   215.2(A)(1)   59

    240 amperes x 125% = 300 amperes

76. C   Chpt. 9, Note 4 to Tbls.   711
                           Chpt. 9, Tbl. 5   717
                           Chpt. 9, Tbl. 4   714

    Size 250 kcmil THHW = .4596 sq. in. x 18 wires = 8.2728 square inches

    5 in. rigid metal conduit @ 60% fill = 12.127 square inches is required

77. B   220.84(C)(3)d.   69

    8 kW x 4 = 32 kW x 1,000 = 32,000 VA

78. D   Tbl. 310.15(B)(16)   154
                           Tbl. 310.15(B)(2)(a)   150
                           Tbl. 310.15(B)(3)(a)   152

    $$\frac{200 \text{ amperes}}{.75 \text{ (temp. correction)} \times .8 \text{ (adj. factor)}} = 333 \text{ amperes}$$

    *NOTE – Size 400 kcmil THWN conductors with an allowable ampacity of 335 amperes is required.

79. B   220.18(B)   64
                           230.42(A)(1)   82

    120 volts x 1.5 amperes each = 180 VA x 50 luminaires = 9,000 VA

    9,000 VA x 125% = 11,250 VA

80. A   220.12   61
                           Tbl. 220.12   63
                           220.52(A)&(B)   65
                           Tbl. 220.42   64

    4,000 sq. ft. + 2,000 sq. ft. = 6,000 sq. ft. x 3 VA   = 18,000 VA
    2 small appliance circuits @ 1,500 VA each   = 3,000 VA
    1 laundry circuit @ 1,500 VA   = 1,500 VA
                           TOTAL (connected load)   = 22,500 VA

    1st 3,000 VA @ 100%   = 3,000 VA
    22,500 VA – 3,000 VA = 19,500 VA (remainder) @ 35%   = 6,825 VA
                           TOTAL (demand load)   = 9,825 VA

81. B   Tbl. 314.16(B)   179

   Size 12 AWG = 2.25 cu. in. x 6 (existing wire in box) = 13.5 cu. in.

   27 cu. in. (total) – 13.5 cu. in. = 13.5 cubic inches remaining space

   $\dfrac{13.5 \text{ cu. in. (remaining space)}}{2.5 \text{ cu. in. (per size 10 AWG)}}$ = 5.4 = 5 wires may be added

82. D   630.12(A)   552
                         240.6(A)   91

   50 amperes (primary current) x 200% = 100 amperes

83. A   210.20(A)   53

   $\dfrac{50 \text{ amps (circuit breaker)}}{125\%}$ = 40 amperes

84. C   Chpt. 9, Tbl. 4   714
                         Chpt. 9, Tbl. 5   718

   1 in. rigid metal conduit @ 40% fill   =   .3550 square inches
   8 AWG THWN = .0366 sq. in. x 3 wires   = - .1098 square inches
                    remaining space   =   .2452 square inches

   $\dfrac{.2452 \text{ sq. in. (remaining space)}}{.0211 \text{ sq. in. (size 10 AWG THWN)}}$ = 11.62 = 11 wires may be added

85. D   Chpt. 9, Tbl. 4   713
                         Chpt. 9, Tbl. 5   719
                         Chpt. 9, Note 4 & 7 to Tbls. 711

   3 in. IMC @ 60% (permitted fill) = 4.753 square inches

   $\dfrac{4.753 \text{ sq. in.}}{.3197 \text{ sq. in. (4/0 XHHW)}}$ = 14.86 = 15 conductors

86. A   Single-phase current formula

   *NOTE – On the primary side of the transformer the voltage to ground is 277 volts.

   I = $\dfrac{\text{Power}}{\text{Volts}}$ = $\dfrac{9{,}600 \text{ VA}}{277 \text{ volts}}$ = 34.6 amperes

87. D   Tbl. 220.12   63
                  210.19(A)   52
                  220.14(K)(2)   63

100 ft. x 200 ft. = 20,000 sq. ft. x 2 stories = 40,000 square feet total

$$\frac{40,000 \text{ sq. ft.} \times 3.5 \text{ VA} \times 125\% \text{ (cont.)}}{120 \text{ volts} \times 20 \text{ amperes (one circuit)}} = \frac{175,000 \text{ VA}}{2,400 \text{ VA}} = 73 \text{ lighting circuits}$$

$$\frac{40,000 \text{ sq. ft.} \times 1 \text{ VA}}{120 \text{ volts} \times 20 \text{ amperes (one circuit)}} = \frac{40,000 \text{ VA}}{2,400 \text{ VA}} = 17 \text{ receptacle circuits}$$

73 lighting circuits + 17 receptacle circuits = 90 total circuits

88. B   215.2(A)(1)   59
                  Tbl. 310.15(B)(16)   154
                  Current formula

15,300 VA X 100% = 15,300 VA
18,560 VA x 125% = 23,200 VA
          Total = 38,500 VA

I = P/E   I = 38,500VA ÷ 240 volts = 160.4 amperes

NOTE* Size 2/0 AWG conductors with an ampacity of 175 amperes should be selected.

89. C   220.14(I)   63
                  220.44   64
                  Tbl. 220.44   64

200 receptacles x 180 VA = 36,000 VA

1st 10,000 VA @ 100% = 10,000 VA
26,000 VA @ 50%   = 13,000 VA
              TOTAL = 23,000 VA

90. C   Trade Knowledge
                  3-Phase Current Formula

1,800 VA x 3 =   5,400 VA (lighting load)
              + 7,206 VA (motor load)
                12,606 VA = TOTAL load

$$I = \frac{VA}{E \times 1.732} = \frac{12,606}{208 \times 1.732} = \frac{12,606}{360.25} = 35 \text{ amperes}$$

91. C   250.66   115
                 Tbl. 250.66   115

    400 kcmil x 3 conductors = 1,200 kcmil

    *NOTE – This installation requires a size 2/0 AWG copper grounding electrode
        conductor.

92. D   430.6(A)(2)   312
                 430.32(C)   320

    FLA = 18 amperes x 130% = 23.4 amperes

93. A   220.56   65
                 Tbl. 220.56   67
                 3-Phase Current Formula

    2 x 10 kW ovens   = 20.0 kW
    1 x 3.5 kW fryer   = 3.5 kW
    1 x 4 kW booster heater = 4.0 kW
    1 x 2.5 kW dishwasher   = 2.5 kW
    1 x 3 kW sterilizer   = 3.0 kW
                    TOTAL   = 33.0 kW x 65% (demand) = 21.45 kW

    I =   VA   =   21,450   = 21,450 = 59.5 amperes
        E x 1.732   208 x 1.732   360.25

94. B   Tbl. 220.12   63
                 210.19(A)(1)   52

    200,000 sq. ft. x 3 VA x 125% = 750,000 VA (bldg.) = 135.3 circuits
          277 volts x 20 amperes   5,540 VA (circuit)

95. C   Tbl. 220.55, Note 4   66
                 334.80   198
                 Tbl. 310.15(B)(16)   154
                 Current Formula

    I = P = 8,000 watts = 33.3 amperes
        E   240 volts

    *NOTE – A size 8 AWG NM cable with a temperature rating of 60°C and an
        allowable ampacity rating of 40 amperes is required.

96. A   Chpt. 9, Tbl. 8   721
                    Distance Formula

   1st find voltage drop permitted. 120 volts x 3% = 3.6 volts

   D = CM x VD = 6,530 CM x 3.6 volts = 23,508 = 91 feet
       2 x K x I   2 x 12.9 x 10 amps   258

97. C   Tbl. 310.15(B)(16)   154
                    Tbl. 310.15(B)(2)(a)   150
                    Tbl. 310.15(B)(3)(a)   152

   750 kcmil XHHW AL ampacity (before derating) = 435 amperes

   435 amps x 1.04 (temp. correction) x .8 (adj. factor) = 361.92 amperes

98. B   220.14(H)(1)   63
                    Current Formula

   50 ft. (multioutlet assembly) = 10 x 180 VA = 1,800 VA total
           5 feet

   I = Power = 1,800 VA = 15 amperes
       Volts   120 volts

99. A   430.22(E)   316
                    Tbl. 430.22(E)   317

   18 amperes x 85% = 15.3 amperes

   *NOTE – When sizing conductors for intermittent duty motors, the NAMEPLATE
            rating of the motor shall be used.

100. B   430.6(A)(2)   312
                    430.32(A)(1)   319

   54 amperes x 115% = 62.1 amperes

176

Copyright 2016   BrownTechnical.org

NOTES

www.ingramcontent.com/pod-product-compliance
Lightning Source LLC
Chambersburg PA
CBHW081821300426
44116CB00014B/2444